FROM A SHACK TO DESTINY!

Bernard Parker
'DIE HOND'

PLAYER, LEGEND & LEADER

AS TOLD TO

Charley Pietersen

All rights reserved. The moral right of the author has been asserted. No part of the publication may be reproduced, stored in a retrieval system, or transmitted in any form or by any means, electronically, mechanically, photocopying, recording, or otherwise without the prior written permission of the copyright owner. It is illegal to copy this book, post it to any website, or distribute it by any other means without permission from the author.

Disclaimer: the purpose of this book is to educate inform and entertain the public in general. The author and/or publisher do not guarantee that anyone following these techniques, suggestions, tips, ideas, or strategies will become successful. The author and/or publisher shall have neither liability nor responsibility to anyone with respect to any loss or damage caused, or alleged to be caused, directly or indirectly by the information contained in this book.

Edited by: Richard Edwards, Beyond The Vale Publishing
Cover design by: Earl Davids, ED Brands & Print
Layout by Boutique Books
Proofread by: Dawn Potgieter
First published 2023

ISBN 978-0-620-98237-5 (print)
978-0-620-98238-2 (e-book)

Copyright:
© Charley Pietersen
© Bernard Parker

FROM A SHACK TO DESTINY

'TIYENDE'
THE WARRIOR SPIRIT

ITEC Tiyende was founded in 2005 and since then has grown from strength to strength. The name Tiyende is a Zambian word meaning *warrior with a strong personality*. A Tiyende warrior is energetic, charismatic, ambitious and focused. Once the Tiyende warrior has a true passion for something, they will give everything for it.

Parker, as Bernard is known in our office, is a passionate individual who gives his all once he is driven to accomplish a goal. He has made a name for himself on and off the soccer field, with wholesome initiatives that warm our hearts.

ITEC Tiyende's vision remains underpinned by values that encourage and drive a high-performance culture, strong corporate governance, a client-centric approach and a focus on diversity and collaboration to accelerate our growth ambitions. Our values of innovation, professionalism, passion and trustworthiness are aligned with the values that Parker lives in the projects he takes on.

As Managing Director of the ITEC Tiyende brand, I have joined with quality people in partnerships, using smart thinking and best-in-class technologies to consistently innovate and react quickly and dynamically to market changes. I view empowerment as a strategic imperative and a vital component of the continued sustainability of the company's operations. Our growth and collaborations are not limited to our service offerings which are communications, security, cloud services, document management and mobility. Our latest collaboration included the installation of equipment to create smart classrooms, making the space innovative and an inspiration for young inquiring minds to be creative and get excited about learning.

Charley Pietersen

Through the Growing Up Without A Father Foundation, Parker has motivated youngsters to grow towards their future ambitions. Words I personally live by are that growth is great, no matter how small, and that great works are performed not by strength but by perseverance. I am committed to keep growing not only myself and the business but also others in their personal capacity. I challenge Parker to keep growing and to persevere in his endeavour to uplift the youth of today to be empowered to be industry leaders for tomorrow.

Simbo Ntshinka
MD, ITEC Tiyende

ACKNOWLEDGEMENTS

ITEC Tiyende; Mr Simbo Ntshinka for partnering with us.

Dr Kaizer Motaung for the Foreword

Mr Benni McCarthy for the Foreword

Mr Mike Makaab for the Words of Encouragement

Mr Sheldon Tatchell for the Words of Encouragement

Me Johanna Parker for her story

Mrs Wendy Parker for the Afterword

The late Coach Mandla Mazibuko for his love for Bernard

Ms Jessica Motaung, Kaizer Chiefs Marketing, and Commercial Director

Mr Vina Maphosa; Cooperate Communications Manager

Mr Freddy 'Sadaam' Maake Kaizer Chiefs supporter

Mr Denzil Bezuidenhout; Mentor and former primary school teacher

Mr Hamish Roskruge; Long term friend

Mr Percy Mahlangu; Friend

Mr Jerome 'Slim' du Plooy; Friend

Mr Emmanuel Kunene; Friend

Mr Reginald Ayer; Friend

Mr David Foster; Friend

Mr Evert Jan Family friend based in Enschede Netherlands

Mr Lyle Lekay; Opponent in the field of play

Mr Vuyo Mere; Teammate, TS Galaxy

Mr Siphiwe Tshabalala; Former teammate, Kaizer Chiefs

Mr Willard Katsande; Former teammate, Kaizer Chiefs

Mr Siyabonga Nkosi; Former teammate, Kaizer Chiefs

Mr Abel 'Chacklas' Shongwe; Friend and Kaizer Chiefs legend

Mr Daniel Matsau; Former striker, Kaizer Chiefs

Mr Johan Erickson; former Thanda Royal Zulu coach and player agent based in Spain

Mr Johan Glenmore; Former Chairman & CEO of Thanda Royal Zulu

Mr Richard Peters Press Officer FC Twente

Coach Stuart Baxter Former Bafana & Kaizer Chiefs Coach

Mr Theophilus "Doctor" Doctorson Khumalo; Former Coach, at Kaizer Chiefs

Mr Muhsin Ertugral; Former coach at Kaizer Chiefs

Mr Gavin Hunt; Former coach at Kaizer Chiefs

Mr Michael Abrahamson; Presenter and sports commentator

Mr Stanton Fredericks; Presenter and sports commentator

Mr Jermaine Craig; Former Media Manager 2010 FIFA World Cup SA

Mr Thabiso Tema; Presenter and sports commentator

Mr Brian Mofokeng; Presenter and sports commentator

Hanley Technologies; Mr Hanley Nyathi for planting the first seed.

CONTENTS

'Tiyende' The Warrior Spirit 5

Acknowledgements 7

Foreword 1: Dr Kaizer Motaung 11

Foreword 2: Coach Benni McCarthy 14

Words of Encouragement: Mr Mike Makaab 18

Words of Encouragement: Mr Sheldon Tatchell 20

Chapter 1: My Formative Years 21

Chapter 2: Education is Key 42

Chapter 3: Ms Johanna Parker, on Her Famous Son 48

Chapter 4: Bernard on Family 57

Chapter 5: The Big Wedding to Wendy Parker 60

Chapter 6: My Time at the School of Excellence 62

Chapter 7: My Time at Bafana Bafana 67

Chapter 8: My Role Model Benni McCarthy 74

Chapter 9: My Time at Kaizer Chiefs 77

Chapter 10: Leader, Captain and Teammate 82

Chapter 11: Spiritual Owners of the Game 87

Chapter 12: Dr Kaizer Motaung, Chairman of Kaizer Chiefs 93

Chapter 13: Crime, Gangsterism, Drugs, Bullying and GBV 95

Chapter 14: Parker's Influence on Others 99
    1. Friends 99
    2. Premier Soccer League Players & Personalities 112
    3. Personalities on Parker 120

Chapter 15: Advice to Young Soccer Players 136

Charley Pietersen

Chapter 16: Mental Preparation 144

Chapter 17: Afterword by Mrs Wendy Parker 150

Chapter 18: Accolades & Awards 152

Article on Cristiano Ronaldo 154

Articles On Parker 161

Author's Summary 195

Pictures 196

Bibliography 198

Bernard the Footballer 201

FOREWORD 1

DR KAIZER MOTAUNG

I considered it an honour when initially asked to write this foreword to Bernard's autobiography and, upon reading the manuscript, the esteem in which I hold the man has only been amplified.

This is one player who has a compelling story to tell and throughout this book, as you read the chapters, you realise that Bernard Parker is a very unique player and a remarkable individual. His background and his career provide an exemplary case study, especially for young people, even those in other vocations, of how, through dedication and hard work, one can rise to become a superstar.

One of Bernard's outstanding characteristics is his indefatigable personality. His roots are in the East Rand, where he spent his youth pursuing his dream of becoming a footballer in the face of numerous tempting distractions, displaying early signs of the steadfast determination that resides in his soul.

His perseverance, allied to his obvious talent, led him to the Premier Soccer League (PSL) and then on to Europe and the Dutch Eredivisie, from where he came back to South Africa as an example of hard-earned success.

When he came to Kaizer Chiefs, he was still young and played for us for about eleven years. The years he played for Kaizer Chiefs were memorable times. He was part of the group of players who won the league and cup twice, at a time coached under Stuart Baxter. During that time, through the strength of his personality, Bernard became a leader, frequently wearing the armband on the field.

Yet, we must remember that it wasn't all plain sailing and there was a time when he received a lot of backlashes from our supporters. When you are one of those who stands out, there is always added expectation on you and when the team wasn't doing well, he became the target of the discontent. It stung him, yet it is a mark of the man he is that he took the criticism as motivation to continue giving his all every time he stepped onto the pitch.

He is a multi-award winner, but his accolades have not gone to his head. He stayed humble and remained a true professional, never absconding or taking liberties as a result of his superstar status. In fact, the more he was recognised, the harder he worked and the better he became. That is Bernard Parker. You'll never hear him speak of his personal achievements, but in the end this book illustrates to us some of the awards he received during his illustrious career. It speaks for itself.

If you think about where Bernard came from – for example, in the chapter where he talks about gangsterism, drugs, bullying, and various other endemic crime – you remember that he is a product of that environment. Throughout this book he passionately advocates for the elimination of such ills from society.

People look up to Bernard as a symbol of the type of leadership we need in our society and I think reading his story will help a lot of people, as well as communities, to overcome the issues that are facing many of us in the era we are currently living through.

Over the course of his career, Bernard didn't only play football. He went on to study and graduate. This is one of the hallmarks of his nature that comes out of the book: making time to study while playing football, with the foresight to consider his future. He went on to marry as well and has marvellous kids, to whom he is a loving father, playing an active role in guiding them through their upbringing. It was not uncommon to hear of Bernard dropping them off at school or collecting them. With his beautiful wife, Wendy he has made a wonderful family, one that serves as a model for our society. Reading through this book gave me a sense of comfort that there are still people who are proponents of the family lifestyle. In that regard, I think the book comes out very, very strongly.

Most importantly, reading the book I'm impressed by Bernard's formative years: how he grew up, as well as his dedication to fulfilling his dream. True to his character as a man of integrity, he rightly credits his mother for her support as a parent, in very difficult circumstances, with a heartfelt appreciation for her part in his success.

About me, as the Chairman of the Club, he obviously shares some fond memories with me and mentions some of the wisdom I was able to impart to him. For that, I am sincerely thankful, and I wish Bernard as a person, Bernard as a family man, and Bernard as a community leader, all the best.

This book will give football supporters – and society at large – something to think about and, most importantly, it will be educational. Bernard Parker's ***From A Shack To Destiny*** is a book I'd recommend everyone to read and to use as a resource to help advance and motivate others to aspire to become leaders in the mould of Bernard Parker.

Dr Kaizer Motaung
Founder and Chairman of Kaizer Chiefs FC

FOREWORD 2

COACH BENNI MCCARTHY

Parker is just one in a million. I admired watching how he turned into this phenomenal player and one of the best South African players playing today. Parker started at a very young age, back in the days when I was still playing, and he was the player who I could see had the potential to be one of the best, or maybe even the best, this country could ever produce because, you know, I saw he had a fantastic mindset.

Look at the great mental players out there today, and Parker is at their level. I give him credit for that, and he simply exceeded all expectations. I knew that he was the player who I definitely felt would go all the way and break that record that I set and become the top goal scorer for the national team if he was given the opportunity to play regularly. It's such a big honour because I don't think there's any player better or bigger to have been able to take out my long-lasting standing record as the all-time top scorer for Bafana Bafana, other than Bernard Parker.

Bernard was the player I genuinely really wanted to succeed me and surpass my record because I think he is a worthy candidate for having his name in the record books for South Africa's all-time top goal scorer. What Parker has done as a football player is unique and remarkable to come from where he grew up in Boksburg, near Johannesburg.

He came from a very tough and difficult environment and to be able to have come out from there and still have a winning mindset takes a lot of guts and effort to achieve. To become the best in South Africa and to compete and play at a high level on the European platform is an achievement within itself and Parker, as a young boy from Reiger Park, went from playing in South Africa to having the opportunity to go to FC Twente in the Netherlands, where he played his best football. He got this education, like me starting at Ajax Amsterdam, playing in Holland. Parker followed the same route as I did. Growing up in the Netherlands and learning his trade there made him into one of the most successful players you can find. He established himself in Holland and became a household name.

I like his mentality and mindset and that makes world-class players. Not great players, world-class players, Parker should be regarded as a world-class player because he managed to do that. Then he came back to South Africa with the same strong ambition. Then he went to Serbia, which is not the easiest country to play in, and played for one of the giants there, Red Star Belgrade. As far as I am concerned, he is the only South African to have done that and probably the only one who could have done that because Serbia is the most difficult place to go and play, and he succeeded. Parker has done that, you know, and so he gained valuable experience. He has European credentials under his belt, and he played in European competitions and there are not a lot of South African players that can say that, so Parker deserves all the respect and credit for achieving that.

Not a lot is said about that in the local media here in South Africa. Come on, give the man credit where credit is due. I don't understand why we cannot call him a living legend of the game while he is still playing. He's achieved more than most players in this country could or can only dream of achieving in South Africa. He is a living legend and is still playing soccer at a high level, showing that age is nothing but a number if you work hard and if your mindset is fantastic. If your mindset is great and if you have an unbelievable family environment, you know, you can play for as long as you can.

He is a very humble guy, respectful, very obedient, and that is incredible. He's been all his life with his wife, Wendy, who is also his pillar of strength, and that's why he has the successful career that he has because he has the best woman by his side. He has his better half and his kids as inspiration, and he shows people that having the perfect family life and a well-balanced life is what is required for success in the workplace. So, congratulations to his wife, and congratulations to his kids for keeping him on the right path all the time.

That should also be something for people, for players, future players and former players to learn from Parker: the kind of human being and the kind of family life that he has set up for himself and how perfect he and his family are together. That's why he was so successful and is still playing at the highest level and giving the best performances that he can. So, yeah, congratulations to that and congratulations for being the perfect husband, the perfect father to your kids and the most perfect football player that South Africa has produced.

I know there are many more accolades and achievements for you to achieve in your stellar career, and I wish you nothing but the best and more, my man. Congratulations once again for keeping the nation happy and giving hope to the kids who come from where we come from. You know that it is possible through hard work and dedication so stay blessed, Parker, and I hope this book is a huge success because that is the kind of person that you are: a successful, good-hearted man, a wonderful human being and a fantastic football player.

I love you, Parker, and stay blessed and all the best with the book. Okay, cheers, your brother Benni McCarthy out.

Coach Benni McCarthy

Teams Benni McCarthy played for: Seven Stars, Ajax Cape Town, Celta de Vigo, FC Porto, Blackburn Rovers, West Ham United, Orlando Pirates.

South Africa national team, Bafana Bafana, where he is the all-time top scorer with 31 goals.

He is also the first and only South African to win a UEFA Champions League winners' medal, playing a crucial role in getting unfancied Portuguese side FC Porto into the 2004 final that was won 3-0 against Monaco. He worked under his mentor Jose Mourinho at Porto. His two goals in the quarterfinal first-leg win over the team he idolised as a child, Manchester United, brought him global recognition. He is currently the striker coach at Manchester United FC, England.

WORDS OF ENCOURAGEMENT

MR MIKE MAKAAB

William Arthur Ward, an American motivational writer, said: 'Greatness is not found in possessions, power, position and prestige. It is discovered in goodness, humility, service and character.'

Bernard Parker is the epitome of what Ward spoke about. I have had the privilege and pleasure of working with Bernard for almost his entire football career, starting with Benoni Premier United, through to FC Twente in the Netherlands, Red Star Belgrade in Serbia, Panserraikos in top-flight football in Greece, and finally to the mighty Amakhosi, Kaizer Chiefs, where Bernard famously plied his trade for 11 consecutive years.

During all this time, 'Die Hond' as he is affectionately known, displayed impeccable professionalism both on and off the field. His dedication to the craft of football was consistently present for all to see. The result of his commitment to the beautiful game is magnificently highlighted by his statistics, both for club and country, during his illustrious career. His affection and care for his family are exemplary – the hallmark of a man of substance. When I look at Bernard, he looks as young as the day I first met him some 15 years ago. He has the same engaging smile, similar but more mature swagger, subtle wit, but most strikingly, a humility that can only come with immense respect for both himself and those with whom he connects. Bernard is measured in everything he says and does. His inner strength in adversity is a quality that is reserved for only the great 'gladiators' in the arena of sport. He seldom verbally strikes back under the flames of criticism, preferring to allow his footballing prowess inside 'the four white lines' to do the talking – and boy does he walk the talk!

Greatness is discovered in goodness, humility, service and character. Bernard has gone about his journey with a good heart, and humble attitude, serving those in his 'circle of life' with a resolute, tenacious and caring character that defines the meaning of true greatness.

I love you, young man. You are much more than a client; you are a son and someone whom I am blessed to have encountered in my lifetime.

Michael Anthony Makaab
Chief Executive Officer / Licensed Football Intermediary and Rugby Agent

WORDS OF ENCOURAGEMENT

MR SHELDON TATCHELL

Dear Bernard Parker,

I wanted to take a moment to express how much you have inspired me and countless others to work hard and overcome poverty.

Your incredible success as a professional soccer player is a testament to your talent, dedication and discipline, and it serves as a shining example of what can be achieved through hard work and perseverance. Your disciplined nature and commitment to excellence have given many of us hope and a sense of direction in our own lives. We admire your unwavering focus on your goals and the way you have remained humble and grounded throughout your career.

Thank you for being such an inspiration to me and so many others. Your achievements have made a difference in our lives, and we will always be grateful for the example you have set.

Sincerely,
Sheldon Tatchell
Founder of Legends Barbershop

CHAPTER 1

MY FORMATIVE YEARS

Positive thinking or dealings attract positive happenings

I am a big believer in the 'mirror test'. All that matters is if you can look in the mirror and honestly tell the person you see there that you've done your best. John McKay

I, Bernard Parker, was born and raised in the dusty streets of Reiger Park, Boksburg. My father Andrew Parker originated from Reiger Park and that is where he met my mom. She originally came from Barkly-East in the Eastern Cape. Everyone came to Johannesburg to look for employment. My mother moved from the Eastern Cape to Johannesburg looking for a job without any place to stay or people she knew in Johannesburg. She met my dad and they stayed at my dad's sister's house in a backroom in Reiger Park, Boksburg. Reiger Park is a coloured township in Boksburg.

I went to Lakeside Primary School from Grade 1 to Grade 7. I was a very busy child at primary school, and you know there were those years at sports day at school when I used to participate in almost all sports activities. I did everything that came up. Leon Schuster, the comedian and filmmaker, came up with a saying *the Gwara-Gwara*, written by DJ Bongz. If Gwara-Gwara was a sport, I would have done that also.

I excelled in a number of sports; the main one was athletics. I did everything from the long jump to long-distance running. Even with my small frame, I tried the shot put. I made it to Eastern Gauteng colours in long-distance running. My speciality was the 1 200 metres. I also did swimming in the local municipal pool, where I did my swimming lessons. I did well in the swimming lessons, and I made it to the nationals for breaststroke. Unfortunately, I didn't make it in the end, and I didn't get my South African colours in swimming.

Soccer always came first. Soccer was always my first preference. I was crazy about soccer, although there was a time when my mother couldn't even afford to buy me school shoes, let alone soccer boots.

One story from my school days was when dyeing hair was the fashion of the day and all the guys were dyeing their hair. I also dyed my hair on the weekend, and I came to school on Monday and the teacher said to me, 'You are not allowed to be in school with blonde dyed hair'. My hair was not that blonde, but it looked bronze. So, I was thinking that I didn't want to go back home because my mom would yell at me; she wanted me to be in school. So, I had to think on my feet.

Luckily, in my bag I had some black shoe polish. As boys growing up we were very meticulous in terms of our shoes: your shoes had always to shine so, you would walk with your cloth in your pocket to make sure that your shoes shone all the time. So, I said to myself, 'Okay, let me take shoe polish and colour my hair black with it'.

I walked behind the schoolyard to the toilets and I coloured my hair black. I then went back to class and the teacher said, 'You're back quickly. Come in and sit.'

At break time I went out again and started playing soccer. You know, when the adrenaline kicks in you forget about everything. I was playing, playing, playing… the next thing I could just see black stains on my shirt and then my friends were laughing, saying, 'Parker look at your shirt!' It was black because of the polish and when I looked up even my sweat was black because the polish was coming off.

When the school bell rang, I was the joke of the day, I just walked right back out of the school gate and straight home. That was one of the funny stories of my primary school years and there were many others. Because

I was such an active and busy boy, I was busy doing everything including cricket. I got the liking of one of the teachers, Mr Denzil Bezuidenhout, and I later became friends with his son, Beuron. He liked children with good manners, and as a child I had good manners and respected people. As a child, we must always have good manners and respect for everyone, especially our elders.

Mr Denzil Bezuidenhout liked my respect and manners, and he welcomed me into his house. Sometimes, I would have sleepovers and sometimes I would go and eat at their house. I really enjoyed it there, especially considering my living conditions. We really struggled financially at home. It was like taking a breather.

He bought his son a new pair of soccer boots, and his son, Beuron, gave me his old pair and that was actually my first pair of boots. I will forever be grateful to that family. He enrolled me with Boksburg FC, a local soccer team, and I played with his son there. I got my Eastern Gauteng colours in soccer. We travelled a lot with the under 10s, 12s and 13s because of the tournaments we participated in. Beuron and I became good friends.

He heard that there were trials at the School of Excellence. He took me and Beuron to the trials. I only played, if I remember correctly, for a few minutes. I think it was less than ten minutes.

Mr Bezuidenhout was very disappointed that we had travelled so far, and we'd only played for a few minutes. According to him, they didn't assess us properly. I thought that I was not accepted, only to find out later in that year that Mr Bezuidenhout got a letter that I was accepted at the School of Excellence, and I had passed the trials. Coach Mandla Mazibuko and Coach Sam Mbata quickly recognised my talent and accepted me at the School of Excellence.

While I was still in primary school, we stayed at Ouma Shirley's house. She was my father's eldest sister. When my father and mother were not together anymore, we were not welcome to stay in Ouma Shirley's backyard any longer. She asked my mother, brother and me to leave. I think that it was only fair for her to let us go, because we had been staying there for free because of my father.

We moved to Bluebell Street Reigerpark, which was not far from Ouma Shirley's house. We didn't stay long at Bluebell Street either because the lady wanted her son to take the backroom where we were staying over.

We had nowhere to go, and my humble mother got help from a friend, Aunty Anna, who worked with her at the local fish and chips shop. She gave us a space at the Ramaphosa informal settlement (a squatter camp) which is next to Reiger Park. We put up our own shack, our two-room shack. There were three of us –my mother, my elder brother, Melvin, who was four years older than me, and me –in the two-room shack.

Credit Picture @EWN Sport

Fortunately, my mother was working in Isando, Kempton Park, at a place where they specialised in stoves, hotplates and electrical appliances. Her income of R500 a week helped to put food on the table.

When I got accepted, I left Reigerpark to go to the School of Excellence in Standard 6 (Grade 8), and it was wonderful. Even till today I say that, if I hadn't gone to the School of Excellence, I wouldn't be the person that I am today. Not only the footballer, but the person that I am. I learned a lot of values, morals, respect, discipline, and a lot of other valuable teachings at the school. Even the students who didn't make it in terms of becoming professional footballers also came out of there with a lot of life skills and have learned a lot in terms of life.

When I came home during the school holidays. I would have no money. All the other guys would go home and receive money from their parents, and the others were fetched by their parents. And then there was me: no money, no nothing. I also wanted to go home to see my mom. I didn't even own a cell phone, so I'd have to call on the landline, and at home there was no landline, so who could I call?

So, communication was very difficult. My mom was not well educated; she didn't go to school much. She didn't know how to get in contact with me but she would just make surprise visits and then, with those free weekends, as young as I was I took the responsibility to get myself home. I can remember walking home from the School of Excellence, Elandsfontein. I walked right through Whitfield, past the East Rand Mall, past Boksburg North, all the way home: walk, jog, walk, jog. When I got tired, I walked, and it was fun. I did it twice, thrice? Again, I can't remember but it was fun.

I can remember a friend of mine walking me to the station. When I was at the train station, I could see the people hanging out of the doors of the train, stealing a lift. I also learned the tools of the trade and I said, 'Okay, that's a clever way I can do it,' and I did it.

When the conductor came, I would just jump off. I did it a few times. When I had some change (money), I would buy myself a ticket, and then some days, when I didn't have any change, I would always find the means to get back to school. I was always on time. I wasn't much of a problem child.

There were a lot of things at the school that were inspiring. Professional teams would come to take some of the boys. Sundowns came and took Sipho Nunens; Ajax came and took Shaun Potgieter; and SuperSport came and took Daine Klate and Richard Rantjie. More inspiring was that we had international tournaments, like the Nike Premier Cup, and three of our players actually got invitations to Chelsea in England. Those things kept my belief alive; those things kept my dream alive, and seeing the guys make something of their lives was the click at that moment when I realised I was a fast learner. I realised that, if they could make it, then I could also make it, and when I made it I could also make a difference at home. God knew that I wanted to make a difference and change the struggling environment that we were living in.

Fast forward to when I was still in Matric (Grade 12) at the school. Coach Sam Mbatha left the school and coach Dan 'Dance' Malisela came in, coach Sam Mbatha went to coach Benoni United. Benoni wasn't far from the school and Coach Sam Mbatha recommended a few players to join Benoni United. At that time the owner was Mr Dumisani Ndlovu, may his soul rest in peace. I can remember sitting in Mr Ndlovu's Caravelle, and he said, 'Come play for me.' I said, 'Sir, when I finish school, I need to look after my family. That is my first priority. It is tough at home, I need to look after my family.' He promised me that he would look after me, so I said, 'Okay.' When I finished school, I joined Benoni United.

While I was at Benoni United, Coach Khabo Zondo spotted me. He was with Sundowns at that time and asked me to come for trials at Mamelodi Sundowns. I said to him that I was playing for Benoni, and he asked if I had signed with Benoni. I don't remember signing for Benoni, but I think my mother signed on my behalf to be registered. I went to Sundowns on trial. Coach Ted Dumitru was the coach at Sundowns at that time. I played very well. I played for the reserves side against the senior team.

The senior team had players like Tso Vilakazi, Gift Leremi, Sipho Nunens and Peter Ndlovu, just to mention a few. It was a powerful squad.

Sundowns didn't sign me. They took my identity document and I needed to get it back from them, but they refused to give me my identity document back. They made me sign a five-year contract on a piece of paper. Starting off with R5 000. That was not sufficient to look after my family and for me to travel every day. After they made me sign the piece of paper I went back to training. They would give me cash in my hand to pay for my transportation.

I took three trains: from Boksburg to Germiston, from Germiston to Tembisa, and changed at Tembisa. I used taxis to go to Chloorkop, every day back and forth. I would leave fairly early in the morning, before the sun came up at around 06:00, and came back late, at around 19:00 and sometimes as late as 20:00.

Falling from a moving train

The School of Excellence was in Elandsfontein, close to Isando, Kempton Park, and my home was in Boksburg. I had to take a train. Actually, I had to steal a ride on a train from Boksburg Station to Germiston Station and then from Germiston to Elandsfontein when we had free weekends from the School of Excellence.

We used to have one free weekend a month and usually that would happen at the end of the month or the first week of the new month. I did not have money to go home, but I had at least something when coming from home. I tried to save that little money and would rather steal the train. That is what we used to call it: stealing the train, getting on the train without paying.

One Sunday, coming back home to school, the platform was empty. It was not busy like during the week, so it was an ideal day and time to steal the train. That was the easiest way to get away with it and get to your destination without paying. At Boksburg station, there was a fence at the station with a hole next to the track. I would run in that open fence going to the platform and wait for the train to move. Sometimes, I would time the train when it came and I would run quickly through the fence onto the platform and then wait for the train to stop. As soon as the train took off, I jumped on before the door closed.

So here I was, waiting on the platform as the train pulled off. Then I ran to jump on. I grabbed one of the rails and slipped. I slipped and fell under the platform, into a little space. I was very lucky not to fall on the rails. The train was already moving, and it missed me by an inch. I survived death. The people on the platform were screaming and crying and thought that I was dead.

As the train passed by, I came out from under the platform. I was so, so, so scared. Everyone on the platform was screaming, then clapping and laughing when they saw that I was not hurt at all. I was alive but in deep shock. I just ran straight off the platform and through the fence. I will never forget that day. I almost lost my life. Today I am grateful that I am alive.

Mr Ndlovu heard that I was training with Sundowns and he called me and said to me, did these people pay you? I said no, but they made me sign a piece of paper contracting me for five years. He said, 'These people are not serious; here is a proper contract for you. I then signed for Benoni United, and he offered me a salary of R8 000 a month. I was excited about that R8 000. I told my mom that I needed to get my identity document back from Sundowns and I went to Chloorkop with my mom to fetch my identity document. They refused to give it back and my mother swore in Xhosa. It was the first time I'd heard her speak like that. She was very upset, and the Eastern Cape came out like fire in her.

We left without my identity document because they refused to give it to us. We went straight to Home Affairs to apply for a new identity document to get registered at Benoni United, and from then on my semi-professional career started.

We used to train at the Sinaba Stadium in Daveyton, which was a long distance from Boksburg.

I took a taxi from Boksburg to Daveyton and then a local one to the stadium. Then, from town to Dunswart to Benoni down through Benoni town to Esihlahleni which was in Daveyton. I was taking four taxis a day. It was stressful and tiring.

The training was every day. Sometimes, we had double sessions, one in the morning and the other in the afternoon. Believe me, I would sleep under the tree at the stadium after the morning session and then, when all the guys jumped in their cars to go home after the first session, I stayed on the ground waiting for the second session in the afternoon. I could not afford the taxi fare to go home and back. I sometimes trained hungry in the afternoons.

I can still identify that tree I used to sleep under, even after they renovated the Sinaba Stadium.

I slept underneath that tree and waited for the afternoon session. After the afternoon session, I would have to run because I had to catch the six o'clock taxi. Fortunately, the club gave us a taxi allowance every day. At that time, it was R30 per day. I would run to get my six o'clock taxi because if I missed it, I would be in big trouble and I would have to run home, which was a long way and dangerous at that time of the evening.

That year, Benoni United didn't win promotion.

The next year, a beautiful goal by July Mahlangu in the 86th minute saw us, Benoni United, moving to the Premier Soccer League for the 2007/08 season. We beat Vasco da Gama 1–0 at the Bellville Stadium on that Sunday. It was our second attempt to challenge for promotion.

We were doing so well at the end of the season, and I was selected to play for the National under-23 squad. I was reunited again with the likes of Daine Klate, the players I had been with at the School of Excellence. I played with Lerato Chabangu, Lebogang 'Cheese Boy' Mokoena, Roben Johannes and Tsepo Masilela. Those were big stars and names at the time. I was the young one among these big boys because they played in the Premier Soccer League (PSL), and I was playing in the National First Division (NFD). That was my first under-23 call-up.

The club upgraded my salary to a PSL contract. I said to my mom, 'Stop working. We've got a little bit of money and I've seen you struggle. You've been struggling a lot. Please leave your work. I will look after you.' So, she did leave her work and, because I was playing so well that season, my contract was upgraded and I said, 'Mom, we are going to a bigger and better house,' and she didn't believe me.

I came across a guy who was an estate agent at that time. He has passed now, may his soul rest in peace. They used to televise our NFD games, and he said, 'Die Hond' (that is my soccer name) 'I saw you on television'. We started to become friends.

I did not know that he was selling houses but, after discovering that he was an estate agent, I said to him, 'I need a house. I need a better place to stay.' He helped me to get a house. I got my mom her first house there in Reiger Park. That area was called the 'excuse me' area because those houses were different from the normal houses. I got my mom a house and she was so happy about it, and I could see that she was proud of me. She left her work, and I worked for her and my brother. She's always been my first love and I always like to see her happy.

Mr Dumisani Ndlovu of Benoni United owned a plot and he had back rooms. Sometimes, if I couldn't make it home after training, I stayed over at the plot. It was very dark, and it was in the middle of nowhere. Mr Ndlovu's mom used to give us food: it was pap and chicken every day. I would know that, if I didn't get a meal at home, I'd get my meal at the plot, and I would sleep over there.

My mother got her provident fund after resigning. She said to me, 'My son, I want to buy you a car. Because you bought me a house, I need to repay you with the car because I've been seeing you struggling all this time. You need a car.'

I said, 'Mom, but I can't drive, and I don't have a licence,' and she said, 'You'd better take this car, even if you're going to park it here in the yard until you can drive. I don't need this money. Even if I'm going to try and save it, it's gonna be tempting and I'm going to eat this money. So, I've got to buy this car now. Let's discuss it, and when you have your licence you can drive this car.'

So, a good family friend of ours went and bought the car in his name because I didn't have a licence. We bought the car with cash. It was a golf G1, and I made it a GTI. It had a 1.3 carburettor engine – entry level – and was very, very slow. I pimped it up, and I made it into a GTI. And the car was just standing in the yard like that.

I said to my mom, 'I can't be walking every day past this car and struggling with transport'. I said to her, 'Let me try driving it'. I scratched the gearbox a couple of times with the gears, but I learned to drive that car within a week. I learned how to drive by myself. I struggled to drive but I came right when I got comfortable, and I got used to it. I was stopped by the police on numerous occasions, got some fines, and was almost got locked up for driving without a licence. So, I made it a priority to get my licence.

We moved to Durban when Benoni United was sold to Thanda Royal Zulu. The team now belonged to Swedish owners, and I started to play regularly. When I was at Benoni United I was not playing regularly. I also became a regular in the under-23 national team and I received my first call-up to the senior national team, Bafana Bafana.

I was a very young player among these big senior players at Thanda Royal Zulu. I used to see these players on television and now we were teammates. Players like Clement Mazibuko, Patrick Mayo (interestingly I played with Patrick Mayo during his prime time, and now I play with his two sons, Khanyisile and Khanyisa), Peter Ndlovu, Ismael Maluleke and Japie Motale. I learned a lot from these guys.

With their guidance, they pushed me to become a better player. I used to humble myself and allow them to guide me. I allowed them to push me because I wasn't talking back or showing stubbornness or attitude if they shouted at me. I kept quiet, even if I knew I was right. I apologised and learned further. I was the guy you could always shout at there, and I would understand if you shouted at me that I was not doing something right.

In my second year at Thanda, at the age of 21, I was voted captain by the players. I scored 10 goals before the mid-season break. The management and technical team were very impressed with me, so they sent me on trial to Sweden at MALMÖ FF. It was my first time flying abroad, flying to Europe. Johan Eriksson was the coach by then. Johan was the son of Sven-Göran Eriksson, who had been the England National Team coach.

I landed at the airport. I didn't know which airport it was; I didn't know what was happening. I landed and somebody picked me up at the airport and they took me to the team offices. It was the first time I saw a world wonder, after Robben Island and Table Mountain. We drove over the sea from the Danish capital Copenhagen to Malmö. It was quite a drive, first over the sea on a bridge, under the sea through a tunnel and then back over the sea on another bridge.

I can remember it was very cold. It was January at that time. Europe was freezing cold and it was my first time experiencing a European winter, and also the first time that I'd seen snow. I hadn't brought any winter clothes with me because in South Africa we only had our normal team jackets and tracksuits and those were the only clothes I'd brought. I wore three jackets to try and keep warm.

I did well at the trials, but the team couldn't afford me. MALMÖ FF couldn't buy me because they were also going through some financial challenges. That is the same MALMÖ FF where Zlatan Ibrahimović came from, the same academy where he started before he went to Ajax Amsterdam.

MALMÖ FF was busy building a new stadium for the under-21 Championship that they were going to host that year and spent their money on that instead of buying me. So, I came home. But it was a wonderful experience and my first time in Europe gave me some international exposure. I came back home highly motivated and inspired. I continued to work hard, and I wanted to go back to Europe because I saw the benefits of the growth one could achieve by playing abroad.

I then continued to excel at Thanda. I was rewarded with my first call-up to the national team, Bafana Bafana. My debut was next to my hometown Boksburg. Boksburg and Germiston are right next to each other, and that is where we played Malawi, at the Germiston Stadium. On my debut, I scored my first goal for our national team. What a way to be introduced at a national level with a scorcher of a goal! That was the beginning of Bernard 'Die Hond' Parker.

I then got an invitation to go to Red Star Belgrade in Serbia, which again was in the January winter break, again that cold and winter season. Because of my past experience in Sweden, I took some Deep Heat to help keep my toes warm.

Red Star Belgrade did not want me to come back to South Africa. They said that they were keeping me because I was too good. They were highly impressed with me and my work rate and qualities. I signed for them, but I had to come back home to get the paperwork and the residency in place. Then I went back to Red Star Belgrade, which is historically a very big club in Serbia. They won the Champions League once in the early 90s, the only time in their history, but they are a very, very big historical club.

I enjoyed my time there for six months, but I had difficulties as they went through some financial challenges, and I didn't get paid for three months. I called my agent Mike Makaab and told him that I hadn't been paid for three months. At least my apartment was sorted but I was forced to use my own money for food. I needed my salary to send money home. My savings at home were getting depleted. Mike Makaab told me to hang in there.

I said to Mike, 'By next week, if my salary is not sorted out, I am going to book my flight back home.' He didn't believe me. Then the following week I went to the bank and withdrew some money, and I went to the airport. I didn't know how to book a flight through the Internet, so I asked the cab driver to take me to the airport to book a flight, and I got a cheap flight. I booked it three days in advance. I returned to my apartment and kept quiet and trained normally. I told Mr Mike Makaab the day before my flight that I was going home the next day. He didn't believe me, and he said that I was joking.

I packed my clothes, and I asked the cab driver to take me to the airport, and he did. At the airport, I checked my luggage in and was waiting for the plane to board. I put on my new headphones and was listening to the beats by Doctor Dre, waiting for my plane to board.

As I turned around, there came the team manager and the club chairman. The club chairman said, 'Hey, what are you doing? You can't go home.' I said to them, 'I told you guys that I'm going to leave if you don't pay me my salary'. They said, 'You can't do this! You can't leave.'

The chairman said that he was going to give me my money immediately and we must drive to his office, and he was going to pay me for the outstanding three months. This was for January, February and March. I said, 'What about my luggage? It is already on the plane,' and he said, 'Don't worry, someone will get it back and deliver it to your apartment.'

I said to the chairman that he must call my agent Mike Makaab to let him know about the arrangements. They called him and Mike said, 'Bernard, please think about it. He promised me that they will pay your money.'

I went with the chairman. I said, 'My bag!' He said, 'Don't worry, you'll get your baggage'. I said, 'How did you guys know that I left for the airport?' They said that the security at the apartment had called the club. 'He told us that you were leaving for South Africa.' I said to myself, 'This one,' referring to the security guard, 'I'm not going to talk to him anymore because he sold me out, I was almost home.'

I sat next to the chairman in the back of his luxury Mercedes-Benz. I couldn't even look him in his face. I just watched the road until we got to his office. We went straight from the airport to his office to get the money. He took money out of his safe and he paid me in cash for the outstanding three months. I had so much money in my bag that I didn't know what to do with it all. I needed to send some of it back home.

I couldn't go to the bank to deposit it in my bank account because if you deposited over €10 000 (euros) into a foreign bank account you were required to file a Report of Foreign Bank and Financial Accounts with the IRS.

I had established a relationship with the cab driver, and he said, 'Parker, why don't you send it through Western Union? You can send €500 a day.' I was sitting with these thousands of euros and could only send €500 a day. I had to walk around with the money every day and go to training with it in my sports bag. I couldn't keep it in my apartment. My locker at training was very safe and I used to keep it there while training. I used to walk with this bag of money every day. I guarded the bag with my life.

'The funny thing about Western Union,' said the cab driver to me, 'is that, because you are a black person, they will think that you are selling drugs and sending the money out of the country. If you use one particular branch every day, it will make people suspicious. Let's send it from different Western

Union branches.' We did just that: we travelled to different branches every day.

I arranged with him to pick me up after training every day to travel to different branches. We even had to drive across the border from Serbia to Montenegro, which was about three hour's drive from Serbia where I was staying. My visa allowed me to travel to neighbouring countries as well. I managed to send money home all the time. My mother then in return deposited the money into a separate savings account in South Africa.

Let's rewind to when I was at Thanda Royal Zulu Football Club. That is where I met Wendy, my wife, at the Musgrave Mall in Durban. She worked at Total Sports by the mall. The funny story about this is that where I stayed was close to the mall where she worked. I could walk there, and I was at the mall every day.

I would get my groceries there, or I would even go to buy socks just to see her at Total Sports. Because I was a soccer player, I would go there to buy tekkies, slippers, socks, and anything else, just to be close to her. I had my eye on her. I saw her all the time and I started to like her a lot. She was so nice to me when she helped me that I kept coming. One day, I would go just for a pair of training socks; the next day I would go again because I wanted to see her, and I would just buy a keyring.

And then one day this one guy said to me, 'You're here every day'. I said to him, 'My brother, I've got a challenge with this one person in your store. I like her a lot and I don't know how to approach her.' I showed him Wendy. He said, 'No, this person is out of your league'. I said, 'No, at least I can try my luck,' and he said, 'Okay, give me your number and I will give it to her'.

The first week, second week and third week, nothing happened. I went back to the mall, and I did my thing all over again, by buying small goodies every day to catch her attention. Her colleague, the gentleman who had taken my number, started to recognise me from the television and said, 'Are you the one who was making moves on Wendy? Are you playing for Thanda?'

I said, 'Yes, that is me who was making a move on her, and yes, I am playing for Thanda.'

We became friends and he said, 'I will put in a good word for you, don't worry'. Then one day she called me, and said, 'Hey, what do you want from me?' I was cool and said, 'I just wanted to be friends with you, nothing more.'

Humble as I am, I said, 'Can I come tomorrow? I'll bring you lunch or something?' She said, 'No, you cannot bring lunch to strangers.' I said. 'Okay, but can I save your number?' I asked her if I could call her.

I saved her number and I started to call her every night. Hey, how are you, how was your day, blah blah blah blah blah? It took us a long while to meet after that. I would just see her at the shop and go. It took us long to have our first date and she said, 'Okay, may I suggest we go for lunch?' That happened a couple of months after we met and spoke. We had our lunch at Mugg & Bean. We started to become friends and from there I went to visit her at her place in the location and then from there things just happened, till today.

Next, let's fast forward to where I was able to rest up well and started to enjoy my football. I started to enjoy my football and then it was, I think, before the Confederations Cup 2009. I played good soccer at Red Star and then for three months again in March, April and May, with no salary after the lump sum payment. I was fortunate to be called up to the national team regularly. I was coming up and down to play for Bafana, so at least I was getting money from the national team to sustain me. We used to have a game every month, because we were preparing for the Confederations Cup 2009 and World Cup 2010. We did well. We played against Spain, and I scored against New Zealand.

I also scored against Iraq. I played very well and that is when I caught the eye of Steve McLaren of FC Twente. He personally gave me a call through my agent and then he said to me, 'I'd like you to come and play for me, no test (trial), just come straight and play for me. You could just come sign.' I said to him, 'Are you serious?' He said, 'Speak to your agent, who can then speak to the club to arrange everything for you.'

I was so happy. My agent wrote to FIFA, informing them about my situation at Red Star regarding the outstanding payments. I was still contracted to Red Star but, according to FIFA, if a player is not paid for three months he can leave as a free agent. Plus, the club will also get fined or have points deducted. Michael Murphy, South African Premier Soccer League attorney, handled the legal side. He took my matter to FIFA, and I was declared a free agent.

Red Star still owed Thanda Royal Zulu for my transfer fees. They had to reverse the sale so now FC Twente took over the outstanding amount owed by Red Star and paid it to Thanda. I joined FC Twente. That first year that I joined them, in 2009, we won the league for the first time in the club's history of 50 years. We won the Super Cup. We had never won against PSV Eindhoven and that year we beat them. We broke a few records that year.

Ajax Amsterdam had Luis Suárez, De Jong, Emanuelson, Eistenberg, and Christian Erikson (currently playing for Manchester United) and they had all the big names in their squad. We managed to beat Ajax to win the league title and we beat them in the Super Cup at their home stadium also. I am proud to say that I am one of the members of the golden generation at FC Twente.

Wendy came to join me in Enschede, east of Holland, where the club was based, I asked her to come and stay with me and she joined me. She stayed with me the year after the World Cup 2010.

To play in the first World Cup in Africa was beautiful, unforgettable and historical. I can't describe that feeling. To represent your country in the World Cup is a dream come true for any player, especially for a boy from Reiger Park, Boksburg, who was living in a shack; that was remarkable. Never give up on your dreams and never give up, no matter how bad the situation might look.

We didn't go far in the World Cup, but we played our hearts out. On 22 June 2010, we beat France 2–1 at the Free State Stadium, Mangaung,

Bloemfontein, with big names like Hugo Lloris, Bacary Sagna, Éric Abidal, Anthony Réveillère William Gallas, Marc Planus, Franck Ribéry, Yoann Gourcuff, Djibril Cissé, Sidney Govou, André-Pierre Gignac, Thierry Henry, Patrice Evra, Jérémy Toulalan, Florent Malouda, Alou Diarra, Abou Diaby. Nicolas Anelka, Gaël Clichy, Steve Mandanda, Cédric Carrasso, Mathieu Valbuena and Sébastien Squillaci. Coached by: Raymond Domenech

Despite claiming all three points and a historic win over France, as the host nation we failed to progress past the group stages of the competition. It was a sad moment in our camp. We were ranked 83rd in the world that year and France 9th. We finished level on four points with second-placed Mexico but failed to advance to the knockout stages due to an inferior goal difference.

The World Cup squad was big before they trimmed it. There were some big names like Benni McCarthy, Steven Pienaar, Mathew Booth, Macbeth Sibaya, Elrio Van Heerden all these big names, and the unknown Bernard Parker.

I thought to myself that I didn't stand a chance of being selected with all these big names present, but I worked very hard. One thing about me is that I am not one of the most talented players but in hard work, you will never beat me. With hard work, I will outwork you. My hard work complements my ability, I would say, and when the final team was announced, I was selected. I was very happy to make the cut. I did not play in the first game against Uruguay, but I came on as a substitute in the second game and I played in most of the games and, if I did not, I came in as a substitute. Against France, I played for 70 minutes. At least I got my World Cup minutes.

After the World Cup, I went back to Holland to my team FC Twente. The year after we won the league, Coach McLaren left and went to VFL Wolfsburg in Germany and a new coach came with his own preferences and personality, and I was not part of his plans. I am forever grateful to coach Steve McLaren for giving me my first overseas break and the opportunity to play for such a great club as FC Twente. The management of FC Twente was good to me and my family, and I am forever grateful.

I was stuck and for the next six months, I didn't play much, then in January, the same Swedish owners from Thanda got me a trial at Leicester City, England, through Sven-Göran Eriksson, who was the coach at that time when Leicester City invited me for trials and Sven gave me his blessings to come.

I went to England, and it was nice. I saw the King Power Stadium for the first time in my life. We trained at the King Power Stadium, and I played in a reserve team match against Aston Villa FC where I saw the big names like Robert Pirez and Gabriel Agbonlahor. Aston Villa was at that time one of the problematic Premier League teams. I had a good time there and then Leicester City wanted to get promoted. They were in the championship, and they were looking at beefing up the squad up when I went there. They were interested in signing me but then they got Yakubu "The Yak" Ayegbeni from Blackburn Rovers on loan. They went for that option, to take him from Blackburn Rovers on loan rather than to buy me out from FC Twente.

I missed that opportunity to sign for Leicester City, but I enjoyed myself in England. Yakubu was available because he had problems with coach 'Big' Sam Allardyce at Blackburn and then he came on loan to Leicester and helped them get promoted. That is how I missed out. I went back to FC Twente to continue with the rest of the season. We didn't do so well. From being champions, we went way down, and the club had to cut the budget they'd spent to win the league and to maintain and retain quality players. I was part of the budget cut.

I went on another loan to Pantsaraikos. I played at Pantsaraikos and I enjoyed playing there. It is in a small town called Serres in the north of Greece, one hour from the big city, Thessaloniki, also known as Thessalonica, Saloniki, or Salonica, the second-largest city in Greece.

Wendy went back home to South Africa; she was pregnant with Storm during the 2010/2011 season. I enjoyed being in Greece. I scored, and I helped the team. Unfortunately, the team was facing relegation, and they were relegated. I wanted to stay but I couldn't. I loved that small town; I loved the people. I couldn't stay because they couldn't afford me. I went back to FC Twente and did the preseason with them. I spoke to my agent Mike Makaab about what was happening and that at that time I was completely down, and out of favour with the coach.

The club asked him to look for another team for me and he said that Kaizer Chiefs in South Africa were interested in signing me. I said no, I don't want to go back home. Please look for somewhere else because I still wanted to play abroad.

I got a call from Mr Bobby Motaung before I was bought by Red Star. I visited the village because Chiefs wanted to buy me. They showed me around the village in 2007. I took the option to go to Red Star and thought I would always come back to Kaizer Chiefs when the time was right. Bobby Motaung insisted that I must come home. 'Come home,' he said.

I did that and never looked back. I joined the mighty Amakhosi and the rest is history. See you in the next chapters about my time at Amakhosi.

CHAPTER 2

EDUCATION IS KEY

*Impossible is a word only to be found
in the dictionary for fools.*

NAPOLEON

I obtained a Higher Certificate in Sports Management from Boston College in 2019 and completed a Higher Certificate in Sports Marketing. I have a SAFA CAF C Coaching License and I am currently busy with Sports Physiology, Exercise Science, Personal Training, and Life-Coaching at the Trifocus Academy.

Nelson Mandela once said, *Education is key; it is the most powerful weapon which you can use to change the world.*

It is important to gain knowledge. It makes it interesting and mind-blowing to link knowledge with what you do in practice on the pitch and daily life. The key to all is a never-give-up spirit.

Most of us have grown up being taught the importance of education. To be honest with you, I hated school and all I wanted to do was to play soccer, but my mother never stopped telling me how education was important for me. 'Parker, soccer has an expiry date,' she always told me. 'You must have something to fall back on when you stop playing one day.'

I said to myself that my job would be soccer and I didn't need an education. I later realised that education goes so much beyond just getting a job, making my mother happy, and getting her off my back. Education is an enabler, and it is power. You obtain a deeper knowledge and understanding of a variety of subjects to be applied to daily life. You also become streetwise and knowledgeable. Education is not limited to just knowledge from books but can also be obtained through practical experiences outside of the classroom. You meet different people from different backgrounds and beliefs. You can learn something from every person with whom you come in contact, from a street sweeper to a CEO of a listed company. Be open to listening and learning.

Education provides you with a purpose to follow, something to strive for, and provides stability in your life, and it's something that no one can ever take away from you. You meet people from different levels and backgrounds. You can communicate with people from different levels of education. It opens up new doors for you. Our youth needs to get educated and make use of all the opportunities that our beautiful country is offering them, something they never had under apartheid.

Youth, please grab this opportunity to study with both hands. You can even land a big job outside South Africa. Playing locally and abroad when not educated can bring a lot of challenges to you as a player. How do you interact with coaches and players? How do you help yourself in a foreign country?

Education provides financial security. Most of our sports people come from disadvantaged communities and when you sign your first professional contract you just want to buy a new fancy car and party. You don't think about saving, insurance, getting yourself some assets, or saving for better days. Soccer can provide you with a great 10 to 15 years, but what about life after that? Education also provides financial security, especially in today's society.

The importance of education is evident when it comes to being self-dependent. If you are educated, it belongs to you, and you don't rely on anyone else other than yourself. No one can take your education away from you unless you give it away by using substances or following the wrong route in life.

Education is the most powerful weapon you can have, and with it you can make all your dreams come true. So, my advice to youngsters out there, finish your Grade 12 and try to study further if you can.

Look at the following players just to mention a few:

Lehlohonolo Majoro: graduated as a radiologist from the University of Johannesburg and has something solid to lean on should he decide to call it a day in the field. He also has a clothing label called Ballojorro. Lehlogonolo invested in some other business ventures.

Neo Maema: 'Being smart and educated makes it easy and fun in football.' – Neo Maema graduated majoring in chemistry.

Most Educated South Africa Premier Soccer League Players
By Southlight (self-media writer)

Making education fashionable: South Africa's educated football stars.

Soccer stars are known for their flamboyant lifestyles. Given the huge sums of money they make, it's easy to assume that they do not need education.

However, some players have proven that even if they make loads of money playing soccer, education is just as important.

Tefu Mashamaite

The SuperSport United defender holds a Bachelor of Arts degree in International Relations and Politics from Wits.

Tsepo Masilela

The Kaizer Chiefs left-back has a higher qualification in business studies, making sure he has something to fall back on as he approaches his retirement.

Jimmy Tau

Former Orlando Pirates and Kaizer Chiefs captain, Jimmy Tau, had a highly successful soccer career.

He has now easily transformed into a businessman and soccer analyst at SuperSport, thanks to his Marketing degree from the University of South Africa (UNISA).

Daine Klate

Klate has a whopping five league titles to his name, making him the most decorated soccer player in South Africa's history. He has an accounting degree to boot.

Michael Morton

The AmaZulu midfielder holds a Bachelor of Commerce degree in Business Administration and Management from UNISA.

Percy Tau

Holds a Bachelor of Commerce degree which he obtained from UNISA.

Brylon Petersen

Maritzburg United goalkeeper Brylon Petersen has a degree in Mechanical Engineering. Petersen is a qualified Mechanical Engineer.

Education is something that's not only needed on a personal level but also on a global level, especially when your ambition is to play abroad. You need to have that confidence to navigate safely and peacefully through the world.

It helps with being self-confident and is a major part of being successful in life. And what better way to gain that confidence than with an education? Your level of education is often considered a way to prove your knowledge, and it can give you the confidence to express your opinions and speak your mind.

Education can protect you more than you know, not only on a financial level, but it can help prevent you from being taken advantage of by knowing how to read and write, such as knowing not to sign any bogus documents, especially your professional contract.

Inspiring quotes on how education truly helped and encouraged me to further my studies while married and playing soccer at the highest level. It helps me to stay focused and balanced in my life.

Education is the most powerful weapon which you can use to change the world. Nelson Mandela

Education is the passport to the future, for tomorrow belongs to those who prepare for it today. Malcolm X

An investment in knowledge pays the best interest. Benjamin Franklin

Education is not preparation for life; education is life itself. John Dewey

Abedi Pele explains why education is important for football players.

Abedi Pele Ayew, a Ghanaian football legend, has disclosed that education is vital in sport.

According to the retired footballer, today's footballers must be willing to acquire new languages and be able to read to understand what is going on in the locker room.

Abedi Pele stated in an interview with the French Ambassador to Ghana, Anne Sophie Avé, that he had intended to continue his studies at college after completing his 6th form, but football activities forced him to drop out.

'Education is extremely important because today the game is scientific,' Abedi Pele said according to GhanaWeb.

He added, 'There is tactical movement before a coach leaves the dressing room. He has to write that tomorrow we have this programme, and you must be able to read.'

'You also have to ensure that you understand everything in the contract that you are going to sign. You have managers, but you must be able to understand and debate with the managers.'

Abedi Pele explains why education is important for football players | Soccers (scorers.org)

Here is what Wendy Parker had to say about her husband.

A dream doesn't become reality through magic; it takes sweat, determination, and hard work. Success is no accident, she wrote on social media.

It is hard work, perseverance, learning, studying, sacrifice and, most of all, love of what you are doing or learning to do. There is no substitute for hard work, 23 or 24 hours a day. We are so proud of you, Mr Parker.

CHAPTER 3

MS JOHANNA PARKER, ON HER FAMOUS SON

I adore his strength, perseverance, smile and fighting spirit. I cherish his hugs; I admire his good heart; but most of all ... I love that he is my son. I thank God for giving me, Bernard. We did not have it easy at all, moving from house to house and shack to shack. His words as a child were always, 'Mamma, don't worry, I will buy you a house one day and sort you out.' At the age of 19, he bought me a house. A place that I can call my home.

'I grew up watching my mother struggle every day. She was only earning R500 a week, so what I saw my mum go through really touched me. When I got my first professional contract, I decided to buy my mum a house. She's happy today and it makes me happy,' said Parker. Parker made the remarks on Top Billing, a South African magazine show on SABC 2.

Bernard has an elder brother, Melvin, and they love one another very much. Big brother is very caring towards his little brother and the two used to protect and cover for each other growing up. They are still close, and they respect each other a lot. I taught him from the beginning that they don't share the same father, but they share the same mother. They respect and love one another like they have one father.

When I met his father, his brother was four years old, and we used to stay on the same street as his father. When Bernard was born, it was like a miracle. He was born in the house and not at the hospital. We had our challenges as parents in the older days – we used to consume liquor and had our challenges, like any other household. I decided to stop it because it was not taking me anywhere. So, I was not a saint at all. I loved Bernard's father, and he was there for both of my sons growing up. We had some good times as a family.

He never treated my eldest son differently from how he would treat Bernard. We had good times with my husband and when Bernard was born on 16 March 1986, it was a great joy to welcome my other son to this world. He was a very sweet boy from birth until he turned five years old. He started to give me tough times then; he was very hyperactive and busy and just wanted to play with older boys. He was not a fighting type of person; he only wanted to play soccer.

As a child, he always wanted to be outside; he always wanted to learn new things, to experience things. I believe that the humble upbringing and the discipline that I taught him have made him the humble and caring person that he is today. He started to play soccer at the age of five years, and he played with big men and big boys taller and stronger than him, but he was solid and strong for a child of five years old. He was truly blessed with a gift in sport.

He was a very naughty child. He used to play with the unemployed men in the street and he would also bunk school just to play soccer. I would worry myself to pieces that these men would hurt him. My husband and I used to be unemployed and, when he sometimes got injured, he would run into the house and kick everything in front of him and we could not afford to take him to any doctors. We would then nurse him at home.

He would come in the house and say 'Ma, come, come hit these guys that hurt me.' I would then tell him that he knew that he should not play outside with older men like that, so it was also his fault. He would get so angry and kick everything that came in front of him.

Soccer was Parker's priority, he used to admire Benni McCarty and Jerry Sikhosana, former striker of Orlando Pirates, growing up. I used to call him Small Benni.

When he went out to play street soccer, he would ask me to call him when Jerry Sikhosana was playing, if Orlando Pirates were playing on television. He only wanted to see how he scored goals; it was always his thing whenever Jerry or Benni were playing soccer.

The day he went to primary school was a big challenge. He always lost his shoes and socks at school after soccer games. It was a struggle. I would grab him by the hand and go back with him in the afternoon after school to look for his shoes or socks because he would have to have them before the next morning for school. We would find them lying there, where he was playing soccer with his friends. They used the shoes as soccer posts and the other kids would pick up their school clothes after school, but he would leave his behind.

I would ask him if he had finished his homework, and he would then say, 'Ma, I finished my homework at the soccer field.' He was just a hyperactive child. I gave him the name 'Diertjie' because he was very busy. One must be careful what one names one's children because he really behaved like a 'diertjie'.

He loved soccer. On weekends when I cleaned the house, I would find plastic balls all over the house; they used to use plastic bags to make soccer balls. Everyone at school knew that all the plastic balls on the school premises belonged to Bernard Parker. Even the teachers knew about him and that he only wanted to play soccer and neglected his schoolwork.

He used to have a friend who would take him out sometimes and sleep over at his place because he never had the privileges like any wealthy kid to be taken out to movies, malls, and so on. He liked this friend a lot.

He used to go all over the township to play soccer and I was there all the way. If he wanted to play in Galeview, we would just take him there. I would have just taken him wherever soccer was being played, and I sometimes neglected my family duties because of this. If his father became angry in the house he would say to me, 'Let's go, Ma; we must just go'.

I got a job one day, a 'temporary job'. We moved away from our house and moved in with different families and I worked for our accommodation and experienced all of that; how I worked my fingers off for us just to have a place to stay.

Bernard travelled a lot with the school when he was at primary school, and he even travelled to Cape Town for soccer and he did very well. He came back and complained a lot because he played against older boys. He said, 'I look older than most of the older players and they complained that I was older than them because of my skills and ability to play'. They won the tournament.

Parker was good in a variety of sports and excelled in short and long-distance running as well as achieving Eastern Gauteng colours in swimming. He was very talented and committed. I think Parker was running away from poverty and the struggles in the house. He turned to soccer or any other sports outside and did not allow the conditions in the house to distract him from what he wanted to achieve one day. He believed in the future and never complained about our conditions in the house but always came up with encouraging words saying, 'We're going to get out of this, Mam, you don't worry. Trust me.'

High school came, but he was not even there for three months before he was sent to the SAFA/Transnet Football School of Excellence at Esselen Park Sports School in Gauteng. At first, he could not adjust to the discipline and routine of the school, and it was very quiet, not according to his liking. Parker was an excellent, hard-working student, despite the conditions that he grew up in.

We later found a place to stay, moving out from staying in the backyard of families. We stayed all over Reiger Park, renting from backroom to backroom.

When he came back from the School of Excellence, I was staying in Ext 5, and his heart was very sore. He'd made a lot of friends and some of them were staying in big houses, but they enjoyed visiting and sometimes staying over by our humble place. Some of the friends just wanted to be with Bernard because they were free from whatever.

There was a teacher at primary school who used to love Bernard. I think his name was Mr Denzel Bezuidenhout. He did everything for him, and Bernard loved him a lot, and still does to this day. Mr Denzel Bezuidenhout guided him a lot and he is very grateful to that teacher. He was also good friends with the teacher's son, Beuron.

When I looked at my small salary, I wanted to do so much for my children, but I could not afford it. I used to fetch Parker every month end from the School of Excellence, and I used to walk from my work to his school because I did not have a car and could not afford a taxi to fetch him. We did not even have a cent to buy food and he would come and sleep in my two-bedroom rental house.

One evening it was raining a lot and around midnight the water came down on his face, and he jumped from his bed and said, 'Ma, it is raining, look how wet I am,' and we moved the bed from the leak. It was not nice at all, and it was at midnight.

He persevered at the school. Bernard left the house at a very young age to go and stay at the School of Excellence. I missed him a lot and wished I could one weekend just go and stay over there because I didn't know what was happening to my child. I prayed every night that the Lord would protect him because it was only men and boys staying there. One day he told me that the place felt like a prison to him. He was so excited to go to this place and on that day when his father came here to drop him off, he was over the moon. I said to him that he must hang in there and not give up easily. Give it a go!

He stayed there for five years; it was not an easy five years. I used to buy groceries for him and for us here at home and I was just making ends meet. I was not earning a salary, but a wage. Bernard told me not to worry because he was going to buy me a house when he went professional. 'That will be the first thing that I am going to do when I earn my own money.'

I sacrificed everything for this child because I believed in him. I saw his potential. There is greatness in him, and I had to nurture and protect that greatness. Sometimes, when I was eating, I would just think and hope that my son had something to eat that night because I knew he was a big eater.

He met great players at the School of Excellence. Tsepo Masilela and Daine Klate were his teammates. It was so nice, you know, when he opened his first bank account because it was one of the requirements from the school that you open a bank account. I bought him all these requirements, you know, like a kettle and toiletries and everything that he needed. I tried my best with the little money that I received to put something in every month for him, something like R200 in his bank account. He appreciated everything that I did for him.

They went and played in the Simba Tournament, and he scored four goals.

He started to enjoy his stay at the School of Excellence. He said to me one day, 'Ma, don't worry about all the money that you spend on me. I will give it back to you one day and even double to reward you for believing in me. Other children in the same circumstances as he found themselves in worse situations, like drug abuse and homelessness but I sacrificed everything for him.'

The day when I was retrenched was a really dark day in our lives. I used to work at Estia in Isando. I worked there for 19 years; at least as it was a permanent job. The day when I was retrenched, he was already finished with school and he told me, 'Ma, people are coming here. It is a team that is trying to sign me.' He said, 'Please don't just say yes, yes to everything that they say. Please consult with me first. I'm going to write on a piece of paper what you must tell them, the demands that I want before I will sign for them.'

Any team that's coming to the house to try and sign him to play for them must go through the same process as put in place by "Mr Bernard Parker".

Ma must tell them the same thing that I'm telling you and what is written on that note.'

Mamelodi Sundowns were the first team to approach us, and they still had his identity document. He wanted to play for Sundowns but was thinking that there were so many players who wanted to play there, and he was afraid that he would not be able to play regularly. Benoni United FC approached us after Sundowns. Mr Dumisani Ndlovu, the owner, convinced us that they wanted him to play for them and that they would look after him.

After he finished with the School of Excellence, he came and stayed at Bluebell by a friend's house until he started working. He signed for Benoni United FC. I attended almost all his games. He enjoyed his time at Benoni United. He was only 19 when he bought me a house. He delivered on all the promises he made that he would buy me a house and look after me. He did all of that. What a remarkable child to call a son. He even helped most of our families in renovating their homes.

He later moved overseas to play for a Serbian side, Red Star Belgrade. He joined Eredivisie side FC Twente in 2009 and was loaned out to Panserraikos in the Greek Super League. During his time in the Eredivisie, Parker won the 2009–10 Eredivisie and the 2010 Johan Cruyff Shield. He came back and joined Kaizer Chiefs in 2011.

He scored a lot of goals; I think over 40 goals. He was awarded the 2013–14 Lesley Manyathela Golden Boot and won two league titles, the Nedbank Cup and the MTN 8 with Kaizer Chiefs. He was used to scoring goals and winning competitions. He felt very bad if Kaizer Chiefs did not win a game or a competition. He would just become quiet. Parker gave his everything to Kaizer Chiefs and he loved the team from the bottom of his heart. His desire was to retire at Chiefs and become a coach one day there or move into management.

Parker is a darling; he is my everything. He took me all over South Africa, Durban, and all the places that I desired and dreamt about when I was struggling. I have achieved all my dreams through my son. His heart is to see his brother becoming something one day and that is something that we all are praying about. Wrong choices made and wrong friends have led to his downfall. As a parent, it is hard to comprehend that one of your children is excelling and the other one is caught up with the world's social ills. It is heartbreaking. I love both of my children a lot. I invested my time in both. We still have hope that he will make a turnaround in his life. Parker is forever grateful to his brother, who looked after him when he was small, who taught him how to read and spell, and who always protected him.

The passing away of my husband, Andrew, on 12 July 2021, has hurt Bernard a lot. He passed away when they had started to find one another.

Bernard married a remarkable woman in Wendy. She even thanked me at their wedding, saying that I have raised a good husband and a real man. I've got two beautiful grandsons, Storm and Skye. I know that they are going to be great fathers to their children one day, just like their father.

Parker is a people person with a good heart. He has helped a lot of people in his lifetime.

Advice to mothers and single mothers

Believe in your children, invest love and time in them, and support them in their activities and dreams.

I bought him a red Golf GTI with my retrenchment money because it was very difficult for him to use taxis to go to training. Mind you, the guy did not have a licence and I think he could not even drive. He insisted on driving to his training on his own so that the other players could see that he was sorted. He came back very happy, saying that the players liked his car.

I sacrificed my last money to buy him that vehicle because he needed transport for his assignment: soccer. I applied for a RDP House, and I am still waiting for it. At the time I was staying at someone's house who passed away and the family asked me to look after the house because there was no one else to look it. I stayed there for almost five years, renting, but also on the other side taking care of the house, I stayed very nicely there.

Parents remember, "It is not over until God says so." Never give up on your children because of the circumstances that you are living in.

CHAPTER 4

BERNARD ON FAMILY

My family is my everything: my wife and my two boys, my mother and brother, and my in-laws complete Bernard Parker.

Every person needs a good family life and family structure. Life can sometimes be cruel and lonely and for anyone it is necessary to come back to a loving, peaceful and cosy home after a long working day or travelling away from home.

I love my wife tremendously, and my two boys, Skye and Storm. My wife is my pillar of strength and number one fan. She will always encourage me to never give up easily, especially when the chips are down. Wendy, you are my 'Queen' and my pillar of strength.

Wendy Parker: 'Bernard is a great father and husband. He is a calm person who enjoys being around his family; therefore, he spends much of his leisure time with his family.'

My children, Skye and Storm, you are the reason I open my eyes in the morning and close them in the evening. I am nothing without you. Because of my upbringing, I told myself that I want to be a present and involved father in the lives of my two boys.

My mother occupied a special place in my life, and I will be forever grateful to her for what we went through. My mother was there when I kicked my first plastic ball and when I signed my first professional contract. 'Ma, you are the best.' She sacrificed herself, her time, and her pension money to buy me my first car, to help me to go to training and not use taxis and trains anymore.

To my brother Melvin, I love you a lot. Thank you for caring and protecting me when we were growing up. Please keep on fighting for your breakthrough in life. Never give up on yourself.

Lesson learned from Cristiano Ronaldo when it comes to family

Cristiano Ronaldo is one of the greatest footballers of all time. He has been an inspiration for many people around the world, including myself.

Born to a poor family, he entered the stage of football and has been ruling it for almost two decades. With five Ballon d'Or awards and many more to come, he showed the world why he is still the best.

There are many things we can learn from him but one that stands out is his love for his mother, who supported him through thick and thin, and his family and children.

Spend Quality Time with your Family

Ronaldo is a family man. He spends quality time with his family, even with his hectic schedule, and he loves to play with his children. He often credits his success to his mother. She has been the backbone throughout his career.

Having a supportive family is a great thing for a person. They are the ones who care the most for us. So, it's very important to spend quality time with your family. Enjoy your time with them, which helps you to relieve stress and helps you to achieve more in your life.

https://winnersstory.com/life-lessons-cristiano-ronaldo/

CHAPTER 5

THE BIG WEDDING TO WENDY PARKER

I got married to the girl of my dreams! My queen Wendy Cherry was now Mrs Parker from 17 June 2012. I am so blessed. We got married in Ballito, KwaZulu-Natal, north of Durban. We had close friends and family attending our wedding. To me, marrying my queen was like a dream come true. I love my wife from the bottom of my heart.

We are committed to one another as per our vows, and we make sure that no one comes between us.

The wedding ceremony was attended by 170 guests at the Braeside Wedding and Functions venue in Ballito.

I spoke to my wife-to-be about fixing a date for the wedding. It was just a matter of finding the right time on the rare occasion when I wasn't playing a soccer match (off-season), so we settled for 17 June.

This month and date are very important to the calendar of every South African. The June 16 Soweto Youth Uprising that began in Soweto and spread countrywide, profoundly changed the socio-political landscape in South Africa. I salute the Youth of 1976 for what they have done for us as a country. They sacrificed their lives to give us the Freedom that we enjoy in this country. I was only eight years old when democracy came to South Africa.

We got married a year before the wedding at Home Affairs, and we officially made it; it was so special in the sense that I was standing next to my queen. I was meeting my queen, and I was going to spend the rest of my life with my queen. The woman of my dreams.

Lessons learned from my marriage are that my wife and I are still laughing together daily; we're still developing ourselves as individuals; and we're still intentionally developing our relationship with one another.

We're still dating, together adventurous inside and out of the bedroom, smiling more than not, and there's no sign of us slowing down. It is healthy to do things together as husband and wife. We're together because we genuinely enjoy one another and we're both very complementary to each other's lives.

Marriage is an opportunity for a man and a woman to lean on one another throughout the journey of life.

Wendy and I are still enjoying our time together because we're always sharing new experiences together.

CHAPTER 6

MY TIME AT THE SCHOOL OF EXCELLENCE

If it wasn't for the School of Excellence, I wouldn't be where I am today. I have such great fun and a great foundation thanks to the School of Excellence. They instilled discipline, respect and a sense of belonging in me. I learned about living with different cultures and diversity. The school wasn't only producing good players but also good men. I am what I am because of the School of Excellence. I can say the school was the cause of the distinction in the foundation of Bernard Parker and it was my best years as a soccer player.

The late Coach Mandla Mazibuko - 12 July 2022

The SAFA-Transnet School of Football Excellence was launched in 1994. The school was widely viewed as the bedrock of football development and so it was. We started with 30 talented and gifted players from all over South Africa – players from diverse cultures and beliefs – and it later grew to 60. I was like the headmaster and father figure to these boys. Some of them came from broken and fatherless homes. I have treated them like my own children. The school has produced more than 30 professionals, including Bafana Bafana stars Steven Pienaar, Bernard Parker, Bryce Moon, Masilo Modubi, Mabhuti Khanyeza, Dillon Sheppard and Daine Klate.

On the academic front, we pushed them hard. We taught them to balance soccer development with academic development. It was tough, but the boys were very eager to learn and cooperative.

When Bernard Parker arrived at the School of Excellence, I immediately spotted the raw, undeveloped talent. He was a tiny little boy and very reserved, but I saw deep inside of him that this boy was a future star and future asset for South Africa who needed to be developed and I was going to give my everything to develop this young man. I was in charge of the School of Excellence. Like a housefather, all the kids from different provinces from different cultural denominations arrived and as a leader and as a father I made sure that I embraced diversity. I made sure that I made them feel at home and comfortable and other players who were already there as senior players to make sure that the youngsters who were coming in didn't feel left out.

I did my best to know each and every player who arrived at the school and, when Bernard arrived, I saw a scared but determined young boy who just needed some attention from a father figure. He was well-mannered and eager to learn. I decided that I was going to give him a shoulder to lean on. As the boys arrived at the school they were from different backgrounds. I made sure that all of them felt at home and fitted in.

In Parker, I saw a lot of untapped talent, although the other coaches disagreed with me. He was a hard worker and eager to learn. I made sure that I developed each boy according to their talents and abilities and I never tried to force my philosophy of football on them. I made sure that I did not tamper with the God-given talent of the players. I just needed to make sure that I developed their talent, and got the best out of them and took them to the next level.

There were some days when you could see that the boys were not used to this environment. They came from different environments. Bernard came from Reiger Park, a very tough environment where drugs and gangsterism were the order of the day and he needed to escape from that environment. He needed to develop into a role model who would go back to his community and influence them positively. He needed to show the youngsters there that there is life apart from using drugs and being part of a gang.

Bernard was born a left footer and I made sure to train him so that he could use both feet easily. He was a hard worker. The more you made things difficult for him, the more he saw that as a challenge to overcome. I never saw him misbehave or get angry. He would take any instructions given to him and execute them 100%.

I facilitated for him to go to Sundowns for trials and he didn't like it there, so he moved to Benoni Premier United/Thanda Royal Zulu; I also helped him to go there. When he arrived there, he worked very hard, and he used to call me to advise him on the warm-up sessions. He was a leader on the field without him being the captain. He would say, 'Coach, I'm giving them that warm-up session that you taught us.' I watched all the games that he played with a big interest.

Bernard is a left-footed player, but we trained him to be versatile enough to use both feet, and you can see that he's comfortable with both feet and most people don't know which is his stronger foot. He is actually left-footed, but he can play with both feet, and he can play anywhere on the field, wherever he is needed. He works so hard and, amazingly, every coach that came to Kaizer Chiefs had him as their key player.

Bernard was groomed, trained, and developed to be the type of player whom every coach would want to include in their plans. His eagerness and willingness to be developed makes it easy for any coach to train him. He is one of the players who has never really disappointed any coach.

I was like a father and big brother to them, and I made sure that when I noticed that the chips were down, I was there for them.

Bernard made us proud when he went abroad. He played in difficult places like Serbia. He played in the Netherlands' tough divisions and went to Greece, and he made it. He is a strong and well-rounded player whom any coach would dream to have on his team.

He is a hard worker, he doesn't talk back, his attitude is huge, as is his willingness to learn. He is a respectful player who respects everyone. I love him and I knew that Bernard was going to become a great player when he moved to Bafana Bafana and did very well.

I always followed his progress from Thanda, overseas, Bafana, and later Kaizer Chiefs, with great interest and I am honoured to say something about this great legend of the game of soccer in his book. Mark my words, he has the ability to play up to the age of 40 years and beyond, because of his healthy lifestyle and work ethic. He had a solid foundation, laid at the School of Excellence. Bernard hasn't forgotten what he was taught. He's taking it all over with him and my last words to Bernard are stay as humble as you are; you are a great sportsman and family man.

'Bernard, you have no jealousy in you; you love your teammates. One can see how you celebrate their successes when they have scored a goal and remain calm even when people are saying some negative things about you. You will deprive yourself of success and you will make sure that other players succeed and shine around you. I know that even after football you will play a huge role in the development of the game and players. I know that Kaizer Chiefs will rope you in one day in their development structures after your retirement. You are a great role model to South African youngsters and older players.

'Bernard Parker, I appreciated that you earmarked me, and you gave recommendations that I must be part and parcel of your book, your history, so keep up the good work.

'I consider you to be the greatest player that even now most youngsters should look up to you as their motivator and role model. You are a great leader. You got the opportunity of leading a big club like Kaizer Chiefs as captain, so that integration of young players with senior players could happen. It is very important, so you've played that part with distinction. I could identify that integration from young to senior, which is good on your part.

Charley Pietersen

'Stay humble like you are. You have achieved so much because you have playing in three different leagues, and you are the only one who has played in the most difficult leagues that I am aware of. I'm talking about the Dutch League in Holland and in Greece and Serbia. You have managed to come out tops out of those leagues. That alone showed to everyone that your grooming was perfectly done, especially your foundation, which carried you up into the senior level, which is a plus to you.

'I'm hoping that you are going to be an advisor and a motivator to the upcoming youngsters. They must look up to you as their mentor. Mentor them with distinction, without fail, so good luck in your endeavours. You are the only one who played in your era with the group of players who have reached this age, and I hope you carry on throughout. So, good luck to you.

'Bernard Parker, you participating in three prestigious tournaments alone was the greatest achievement any player dreams about. You did it!

'You participated in the national team, Bafana Bafana' when they played in the Confederation Cup in 2009, the World Cup in 2010 in South Africa then furthermore you participated in the Africa Cup of Nations Tournament in 2013.

So, keep up the good work' and I'm proud of you. You showed the grounding, the foundation that was perfectly done without any shortcuts in laying a perfect and quality foundation in you. Stay blessed and safe.

I wish you all the best with your book, playing career and future endeavours. Thank you for allowing me to impart what I have learned over the years about your development.

Coach Mandla Mazibuko
Former Coach, School of Excellence

CHAPTER 7

MY TIME AT BAFANA BAFANA

Picture credit to bing.com/images

Bafana: 72 Caps, 23 Goals

'Bernard Parker follows the legendary striker and mentor, Benni McCarthy's, level on 23 goals scored from 72 appearances to his name.'

I scored twice against Botswana in an international friendly in a 4–1 win in Durban, netting a clinical free kick in the process.

In one of the African Nations Cup group stage qualifiers, I scored both goals, one for Bafana and an own goal I wish to forget. It was against Ethiopia in Addis Ababa.

I made my national team debut against Malawi in 2007 and scored my first goal in 2008 against Malawi.

Who are Bafana Bafana's top scorers?

1. Benni McCarthy – 31
2. Shaun Bartlett – 29
3. **Bernard Parker – 23**
4. Katlego Mphela – 23
5. Phil Masinga – 18
6. Siyabonga Nomvethe – 15
7. Sibusiso Zuma – 13
8. Percy Tau – 13
9. Tokelo Rantie – 12
10. Siphiwe Tshabalala – 12

My achievements playing for Bafana Bafana.

2009 Confederations Cup and 2010 World Cup.

Representing my country two times in the Africa Cup of Nations (AFCON) in 2013 and 2015 was also one of the highlights of my career. On 17 June 2009, I scored both goals in a 2–0 win over New Zealand in the Confederations Cup and was also voted the Man of the Match in that game.

On 19 November 2013, I scored the only goal for Bafana against a full-strength Spanish national team, who were current world champions at that time. What a stunning goal, even if I have to say it myself. I scored it by chipping the ball over the great Víctor Valdés in the 56th minute in a 1–0 shock win over the then-world and European Champions Spain at Soccer

City (FNB Stadium), where they won the World Cup in 2010 by defeating the Netherlands.

I won the top goal scorer award at the 2014 African Nations Championship with four goals from three group matches. It was an honour to represent and score goals for my country.

National Team Games Statistics

No. Date – Match – Score – Competition, Notes

1. **26.05.07-Somhlolo v Malawi 0-0 Cosafa Castle Cup Group B semifinal scored in the post-match penalty shootout.**
2. 27.05.07-Somhlolo v Mauritius 2-0 Cosafa Castle Cup Group B final replaced by Lewis in the 76th minute.
3. 24.10.07-Bloem v Zambia 0-0 Cosafa Castle Cup final replaced by Chenene in the 70th minute.
4. 20.11.07-Durban v Canada 2-0 friendly international
5. 11.03.08-Germiston v Zimbabwe 2-1 friendly international came on for Ngwenya in the 80th minute.
6. 26.03.08-Pretoria v Paraguay 3-0 friendly international came on for Tshabalala in the 82nd minute.
7. 09.09.08-Pretoria v Guinea 0-1 friendly international came on for Moriri in the 87th minute.
8. **30.09.08-Germiston v Malawi 3-0 friendly international two goals; replaced by Schalkwyk, 82nd minute.**
9. 11.10.08-Malabo v Equatorial Guinea 1-0 World Cup group four qualifier came on for Nkosi in the 75th minute.
10. **15.10.08-Bloem v Ghana 2-1 friendly international came on for Nkosi in the 64th minute to score the winner.**

11. **19.11.08-Rustenburg v Cameroon 3-2 friendly international replaced Nkosi in 39th min and got winning goal.**
12. 11.02.09-Polokwane v Chile 0-0 friendly international came on for Nkosi at half-time
13. **28.03.09-Phokeng v Norway 2-1 friendly international scored an early goal; replaced by Moriri in the 83rd minute.**
14. 31.03.09-Lausanne v Portugal 0-2 friendly international replaced by Mashego in the 78th minute.
15. 06.06.09-Orlando v Poland 1-0 friendly international Replaced by Van Heerden in the 88th minute.
16. 14.06.09-Jo'burg v Iraq 0-0 FIFA Confederations Cup Replaced by Pienaar in the 85th minute.
17. **17.06.09-Rustenburg v New Zealand 2-0 FIFA Confederations Cup scored twice; replaced by S Tshabalala in the 81st minute.**
18. 20.06.09-Bloem v Spain 0-2 FIFA Confederations Cup replaced by S Tshabalala in the 93rd minute.
19. 25.06.09-Jo'burg v Brazil 0-1 FIFA Confederations Cup
20. 28.06.09-Rustenburg v Spain 2-3 FIFA Confederations Cup
21. 05.09.09- Leverkusen v Germany 0-2 friendly international replaced by Khenyeza in the 60th minute.
22. 08.09.09- Limerick v Republic of Ireland 0-1 friendly international replaced by Tshabalala in the 64th minute.
23. 10.10.09-Oslo v Norway 0-1 friendly international replaced by Cale in the 72nd minute.
24. 14.11.09-Port Elizabeth v Japan 0-0 friendly international came on for McCarthy in the 74th minute.
25. 18.11.09-Bloemfontein v Jamaica 0-0 friendly international came on for Tshabalala in the 81st minute.
26. **16.05.10-Mbombela v Thailand 4-0 friendly international came on for Moriri in the 63rd minute and scored.**

27. 24.05.10-Jo'burg v Bulgaria 1-1 friendly international came on for Modise in the 69th minute.
28. 31.05.10-Polokwane v Guatemala 5-0 friendly international came on for Tshabalala in the 70th minute.
29. 05.06.10-Pretoria v Denmark 1-0 friendly international came on for Modise in the 77th minute.
30. 11.06.10-Jo'Burg v Mexico 1-1 2010 FIFA World Cup came on for Pienaar in the 83rd minute.
31. 22.06.10-Bloemfontein v France 2-1 2010 FIFA World Cup replaced by Nomvete in the 68th minute.
32. 11.08.10-Jo'burg v Ghana 1-0 friendly international.
33. **04.09.10-Nelspruit v Niger 2-0 2012 Nations Cup qualifier scored.**
34. 10.10.10-Freetown v Sierra Leone 0-0 2012 Nations Cup qualifier replaced by Gould in the 90th minute.
35. 17.11.10-Cape Town v USA 0-1 friendly international replaced by Erasmus in the 88th minute.
36. 09.02.11-Rustenburg v Kenya 2-0 friendly international replaced by Serero in the 71st minute.
37. 26.03.11-Johannesburg v Egypt 1-0 2012 Nations Cup qualifier replaced by Segolela in the 61st minute.
38. 14.05.1-Dar es Salaam v Tanzania 1-0 friendly international replaced by Majoro in the 67th minute.
39. 05.06.11-Cairo v Egypt 0-0 2012 Nations Cup qualifier caution; replaced by Segolela in the 74th minute.
40. 10.08.11-Johannesburg v Burkina Faso 3-0 friendly international came on for Mphela in the 68th minute.
41. 04.09.11-Niamey v Niger 1-2 2012 Nations Cup qualifier replaced by B Khumalo in the 90th minute.
42. 08.10.11-Nelspruit v Sierra Leone 0-0 2012 Nations Cup qualifier replaced by Letsholonyane in the 64th minute.

43. 07.09.12-Sao Paolo v Brazil 0-1 friendly international came on for Benni McCarthy in the 44th minute.
44. **11.09.12-Mbombela v Mozambique 2-0 friendly international scored twice**
45. 12.10.12-Warsaw v Poland 0-1 friendly international replaced by Ndlovu in the 68th minute.
46. 16.10.12-Nairobi v Kenya 2-1 friendly international replaced by Fransman in the 90th minute.
47. 14.11.12-Jo'burg v Zambia 0-1 friendly international replaced by Erasmus at halftime.
48. 08.01.13-Cape Town v Norway 0-1 friendly international came on for Chabangu in the 53rd minute.
49. 12.01.13-Johannesburg v Algeria 0-0 friendly international.
50. 19.01.13-Johannesburg v Cape Verde 0-0 African Nations Cup Finals Group A.
51. 23.01.13-Durban v Angola 2-0 African Nations Cup Finals Group A.
52. 27.01.13-Durban v Morocco 2-2 African Nations Cup Finals Group A replaced by Letsholonyane in the 76th minute; caution
53. 02.02.13-Durban v Mali 1-1 African Nations Cup finals quarterfinal replaced by Tshabalala in the 106th minute.
54. **23.03.13-Cape Town v Central African Republic 2-0 World Cup Group A qualifier scored.**
55. 02.06.13-Maseru v Lesotho 2-0 friendly international caution.
56. **08.06.13-Yaounde v Central African Republic 3-0 World Cup Group A qualifier scored and then replaced by Mashego in the 63rd minute.**
57. **16.06.13-Addis Ababa v Ethiopia 1-2 World Cup Group A qualifier scored at both ends.**
58. 14.08.13-Durban v Nigeria 0-2 friendly international replaced by Manyama in the 80th minute.

59. 17.08.13-Johannesburg v Burkina Faso 2-0 friendly international
60. **07.09.13-Durban v Botswana 4-1 World Cup Group A qualifier scored twice, free-kick and penalty.**
61. **10.09.13-Orlando v Zimbabwe 1-2 friendly international scored.**
62. 11.10.13-Agadir v Morocco 1-1 friendly international replaced by Letsholonyane in the 83rd minute.
63. 15.11.13-Lobamba v Swaziland 3-0 friendly international replaced by Manqele in the 62nd minute.
64. **19.11.13-Johannesburg v Spain 1-0 friendly international scored; replaced by Patosi in the 89th minute.**
65. **11.01.14-Cape Town v Mozambique 3-1 CHAN finals scored twice, one a penalty**
66. **15.01.14-Cape Town v Mali 1-1 CHAN finals scored a penalty.**
67. **19.01.14-Cape Town v Nigeria 1-3 CHAN finals scored a penalty.**
68. 05.03.14- Johannesburg v Brazil 0-5 friendly international replaced by Patosi in the 62nd minute.
69. 04.01.15-Orlando v Zambia 1-0 friendly international came on for Ndulula in the 44th min.
70. 10.01.15-Libreville v Cameroon 1-1 friendly international replaced by S.Vilakazi in the 54th minute.
71. 23.01.15-Mongomo v Senegal 1-1 African Nations Cup Group C came on for Phala in the 67th minute.
72. 27.01.15-Mongomo v Ghana 1-2 African Nations Cup Group C came on for Ndulula in the 85th minute.

CHAPTER 8

MY ROLE MODEL BENNI MCCARTHY

Picture credit to KickOff Magazine

Coach Benni, you have been my role model since I started to play professional football. My room was full of your action pictures. My mother even called me 'Little Benni' in the house.

I watched your first national appearance for Bafana Bafana in 1997 against the Netherlands, and I was only 11 years old when South Africa lost to the Netherlands by two goals. I was shouting for you. Win or no win, you represented South Africa very well.

You also represented South Africa at the under-23 level, and I followed your progress all the way. You made your senior debut in 1997 against the Netherlands and scored your first international goals on 16 February 1998.

I watched you score four times in 13 minutes against Namibia at the 1998 African Cup of Nations, I went crazy when you demolished Namibia. You were in the 18-yard area.

My heart was in pieces when you temporarily retired from international football in 1999. My dream was to one day play alongside you for our National Team or overseas. You came back two years later, which kept my dream possible and alive, and you scored at the 2002 FIFA World Cup in a 3–2 loss to Spain. You are a great role model and leader.

Eventually, my dream came true, and I got the opportunity to share the dressing room and the field with you for Bafana Bafana and you inspired me to limitlessness. I also played against you in the derbies of all derbies, the Soweto Derby. You in Orlando Pirates colours and me in Kaizer Chiefs colours. That was a big moment for me.

I followed you as a player, coach, husband and father. Despite all the challenging times that you have faced in life, you are a man with a high level of determination to get to the top. Your contribution to imparting and raising the younger generation of footballers like me and many others without hope has been immense. I am still looking up to you, which is why I am starting to empower myself in the coaching field and have recently completed my SAFA CAF C License.

Benni McCarthy went on to become Bafana's all-time top scorer with 31 goals in 80 games, and the only South African to win the UEFA Champions League with FC Porto in 2004. He is currently the striker coach for Manchester United FC, one of the biggest soccer teams in the world.

Times Live SOCCER

Confirmed: Manchester United appoint Benni McCarthy

31 July 2022 - BY MARC STRYDOM

Manchester United has confirmed the appointment of Bafana Bafana legend Benni McCarthy as one of the club's three first-team coaches, to serve under new head coach Erik ten Hag.

United tweeted late on Saturday night: 'Welcoming a new face to our coaching team. Great to have you on board @BenniMcCarthy17.'

The club said in a statement: 'Manchester United boss Erik ten Hag has added to his backroom team with the appointment of Benni McCarthy as a first-team coach.

'The former SA striker was a boyhood Reds fan and scored twice against us for Porto in the 2003/04 Champions League knockout stages.

'The ex-forward will specialise in coaching attacking plays and positioning.

'The coaching team is now in place ahead of the start of the 2022–23 season, with Brighton & Hove Albion visiting Old Trafford on Sunday, August 7 in our Premier League opener.

'Ten Hag will work closely with assistants Mitchell van der Gaag and Steve McClaren, with Benni slotting in alongside Eric Ramsay and Darren Fletcher as coaches. Former midfielder Fletcher also has a wider remit as technical director, overseeing the path from the academy to the first team, plus players out on loan.

'Richard Hartis and Craig Mawson are the goalkeeping coaches.' Everybody would like to extend a warm welcome to Benni upon joining the club. 'Confirmed: Manchester United appoint Benni McCarthy' (timeslive.co.za).

CHAPTER 9

MY TIME AT KAIZER CHIEFS

Picture Credit Kaizer Chiefs

Kaizer Chiefs debut: 28 July 2011 against Pirates in the Carling Black Label Cup.

Chiefs 2 Bidvest Wits 1 (7 August 2011).

MTN 8 Quarterfinal, I got my first Chiefs goal against Wits in 2011, and my last goal scored for Chiefs was against Moroka Swallows on 21 May 2021.

I scored the all-important goal in the group stages of the game during their CAF Champions League clash against Wydad Casablanca at FNB Stadium in Johannesburg on a Saturday in April 2021, to qualify Kaizer Chiefs for the knockout stages.

I spent 11 years at the club, playing **359** matches, scoring **62** goals, provided **40** assists and winning two league titles and two cups.

I was Kaizer Chiefs All-time top scorer in the PSL Era from 1996–97 in all competitions. I am currently Chiefs' all-time top scorer in the PSL Era, when I scored a brace in a 2–1 win over SuperSport United in a league game on 24 October 2021 away from home. I scored 12 goals in 28 league games in the 2012–13 season, as Kaizer Chiefs won their first league title in seven years.

I also scored four goals in Kaizer Chiefs' opening league game of the 2012–13 season, as Kaizer Chiefs defeated AmaZulu 6–0, Kaizer Chiefs' biggest win of the PSL era in a league game.

I played in 30 Soweto Derbies, one of the biggest achievements in any player's life, and captained Kaizer Chiefs in the Champions League final in 2020.

On my arrival at Kaizer Chiefs Village, Naturena, I said, 'Joining Kaizer Chiefs is a realisation of a childhood dream. I am happy to be here, and I am going to give my 150% every time I get to don the Gold and Black jersey.' The feeling is still mutual. I love the club, I love the badge, I love our supporters, and I love our management.

I want to thank Mr Bobby Motaung and the whole Kaizer Chiefs management for believing in me. Bobby followed my progress and always gave me a call to remind me that I belong to the Kaizer Chiefs' family.

Mr Bobby Motaung hunted me for a long time. I honour and respect Bobby a lot and we had a great brotherly relationship. I understand him and he understands me. He followed my progress, and he even called me to congratulate me when I scored a brace against New Zealand during the FIFA Confederations Cup held in South Africa in 2009.

I also salute Ms Jessica Motaung, marketing and commercial director, for her professionalism in dealing with players. She made things easy for me at Kaizer Chiefs. I believe that Ms Jessica Motaung has changed a lot of things and brought a lot of spark to South African Football, and with her knowledge and energy South African football and women's football can gain a lot from her.

Kaizer Motaung Jnr, my fellow striking partner, your sharpness and vision on the field of play always amaze me. 'Aweh, Bra.'

I used to work very hard and every goal that I scored was rehearsed at training and mentally. I played abroad for big and small teams for many years as a professional player and always gave my 150%. Go for 150% and land at 110%, that was and is still my motto when it comes to games and matches.

The structure at Kaizer Chiefs is at the same level as most overseas teams. The set-up at the Village is world-class in the way they handle their players. It is expected from Kaizer Chiefs players to behave well and professionally on and off the field.

We must respect the badge and the architect of Kaizer Chiefs, Dr Kaizer Motaung. We need to keep the slogan alive as players wherever we go: 'Love and Peace'.

Kaizer Chiefs was formed by a great visionary leader, Dr Kaizer Motaung. Someone I regard as a great role model and a father figure in my life.

Dr Kaizer Motaung was like a father to me and many players. For the past 11 years, I've looked up to him as a father. I am what I am as a man because of men like Dr Kaizer Motaung and many others who influenced my life. They helped shape me into the man and father I am today.

I always wanted to repay him by scoring goals and winning trophies for him – this man has sacrificed everything in his life to build a team like Kaizer Chiefs. He created a lot of employment and millionaire players.

I have been with the mighty Amakhosi for 11 years. The best times of my career and life. Great players played for this great team, and it is an honour to be counted among the greats of Teenage Dladla, Patrick 'Ace' Ntsoelengoe, Doctor Khumalo, Shakes Kungwane, Zebulon 'Sputla' Nhlapo, Abel Shongwe, Marks Maponyane, Ace Khuse, Howard Freeze, Fani Madida, Shane MacGregor, Neil Tovey, Thabo Mooki, Jacob Tshisevhe, Tsepo Molatedi, Thabang Lebese, Siyabonga Nkosi, Fabian McCarthy, Derek Spencer, Itumeleng Khune, Willard Katsande, and Siphiwe Tshabalala just to mention a few.

I scored 62 goals in over 359 competitive matches for Amakhosi – and am currently the club's all-time top goal scorer in the PSL to date.

Behind me is another true legend and friend, Siphiwe Tshabalala, with 58 goals. He inspired me to do my best and be the best.

We lifted four trophies between 2013 and 2015. We have lifted two league titles and two cup trophies, namely the Nedbank Cup and MTN 8. I was instrumental in scoring the only goal of the game against SuperSport United in the 2013 Nedbank Cup final.

My biggest achievement at Kaizer Chiefs was to play in a total of 30 Soweto Derbies against Orlando Pirates. That's unbelievable. Kaizer Motaung Jnr presented me with a Kaizer Chiefs shirt with the number 30 printed on the back. I was very emotional and could not hold back my tears. That was a real surprise for me. I did not expect that.

Naturena Chiefs Village was home for me and my family for 11 years and I will cherish it for the rest of my life.

My time to move on and make way for younger Bernard Parkers was not the easiest time of my life and it felt that I left the best part of my playing days and life at Naturena.

When your time has arrived to move on, do it with dignity and respect. I have learned in life, and especially in football, to never say never and never burn your bridges! It was great and special to play for the Mighty Amakhosi. Kaizer Chiefs will soon be counted as one of the best teams in South Africa and Africa. Watch this space.

MESSAGE FROM MS JESSICA MOTAUNG, KAIZER CHIEFS MARKETING AND COMMERCIAL DIRECTOR

The first word that comes to mind when it comes to Bernard Parker is that he is a true 'gentleman'.

He is an amazing leader, both on and off the pitch. I had many interactions with Bernard over the years and my assessment of him is that he is always very professional. He took his duties as club captain and one of the leaders of the club during his tenure very seriously and was whole-heartedly committed to the Kaizer Chiefs brand.

He represented us with distinction and was truly 'A Khosi for Life' – a special individual both on and off the field.

He was also very dedicated to our work with our sponsors and did a lot of work with us on the Corporate Social Investment projects of the club.

He was a rare breed who, with his international experience at both club and national team level, truly understood the footballing landscape and who had a good grasp of football as a business.

It was these qualities, as well as his considerable football acumen, that ensured he could stay with the club for over 11 years and could make nearly 300 appearances for the club and lead us to many titles on the pitch.

I enjoyed working with him. While he was hardworking, he was also lots of 'fun' and a very positive part of Chiefs' establishment during a wonderful career with the club.

I am proud that he was part of the Kaizer Chiefs' family for so many years. I worked closely with him – and worked with him very well.

Charley Pietersen

CHAPTER 10

LEADER, CAPTAIN AND TEAMMATE

To be selected to captain a team, especially a team of Chiefs' calibre and magnitude, is an honour that comes with a lot of accountability and responsibility. The responsibility is so huge you will notice that most players perform very well and later, after being made captain, their form drops. It is not easy at all.

It is not an easy position to lead and play at the same time. You are under scrutiny and the responsibility is enormous. You need to be there for your teammates at all times, and also make sure that you don't lose yourself as a player and person.

You become target number one for referees who perceive you as arrogant if you question certain decisions taken by them that you and the team are not happy with. I sometimes feel that referees ignore giving captains the opportunity to ask them what we, the players, have done wrong when they caution them.

I believe that as a team and captain, we must always be respectful to our supporters. The captain must always lead his teammates in saluting or applauding the cheers of our supporters before and after the game. Win or lose.

A captain must always encourage his teammates about teamwork and good sportsmanship. Treat your opposition team with respect, especially at your home ground. Respect must not be seen as meaning that we are scared of them, but just good sportsmanship. The captain must remind his teammates that home games are our guaranteed three points, period. We dare not lose, especially in front of our beloved supporters.

The medical teams, paramedics, and ball boys must also be respected as well.

Things a good captain should be doing all the time. They are sometimes not easy, but they must be done.

1: Walk the talk

A good captain has to walk the talk. It is no good asking the team to do things that you are not prepared to do yourself. Leading by example inspires the rest of the team to do what you do. It helps to strengthen the team when they know that the captain is willing to make the same sacrifices they are making. Leading by example makes it clear to everyone that the team is working together to win every game. Don't forget that you are the eyes and ears of the technical team on the field of play.

2: Inspire teammates

Don't criticise your teammates when they do something wrong. Nobody is perfect, and nobody gets it right all the time. Shouting at someone when they make a mistake during the game does nobody any good and can result in the player getting nervous and making more mistakes. Be each other's keepers on the field of play. There is a saying 'I am my brother's keeper'.

3: Lead on the field

The coach cannot coach on the field of play while the game is on. He cannot even coach from the sidelines. Once the team is on the field of play, the coach's job has pretty much been done for the moment. The captain is usually a central defender, central midfielder, striker, or goalkeeper because, from those positions, he can see the whole field and can organise the team. The captain needs to remember each teammate's playing styles, strengths and weaknesses, as well as the coach's instructions, and communicate this while on the field of play. Keep the team spirit high, win or lose.

4: Creating strong relationships

In a good team, teammates know and trust each other. The team captain should be the person that they trust most, and to achieve this you have to work hard at building a strong relationship with each teammate and encourage them to be friends not only with you but with their fellow teammates. The better everyone knows, understands and trusts each other, the stronger the bonds between teammates and the better the team will perform.

5: Be there for your teammates

You need to notice what is going on with your teammates. If they are playing badly, it may be because of something happening in their lives. Even if they are still playing to form, they may seem unhappy and it is up to the team captain to observe these things and follow up on them with a question like, 'Is everything going okay with you at the moment?' 'How are things at home?' This will show that you care. By showing empathy towards what your teammates are going through, you help to build strong relationships and gain your teammates' respect.

6: Stay serene

As the captain, you have to keep your mind calm and serene. Even when everyone else is ready for a fight, you have to stay calm and try to find the best solution. Even when a referee has made a bad call, or one of the opponent players has fouled your teammate, you need to keep a cool head and try to make them show some respect. Even in the hottest moments, you have to be cold-blooded. Remember if the referee has issued a card to your teammate his decision is final, we don't have a Video Assistant Referee (**VAR**) system to verify. An argument won't change the decision taken by the referee. Please leave him alone.

7: Inspire motivate and stay positive

As the team captain, it is your responsibility to maintain the energy and positivity of the team. Even when nobody else sees any hope of winning the game, you must inspire and motivate every teammate and let them know that anything is still possible. As a team captain, you should be positive all the time and everywhere, not only when playing a game. In the game, no matter how badly your team is losing you need to keep up a positive attitude – and then sometimes miracles are pulled off.

8: Treating the referee with respect

Technically, the captain is the only member of the team who is allowed to talk to the referee during a soccer game, although in practice this is not what happens. 'Be careful, certain referees hold grudges.' 'It is just a joke.' Whatever the case, as the captain, it is your responsibility to communicate on the team's behalf. It is a good idea to always defend the referee. This gets him on your side since referees like to feel respected and protected. The very last thing you should do is lose your temper and get into a shouting match with the referee. (Don't try anything silly with referees like Ms Akhona Makalima and Mr Victor Gomes: they will give you the whistle to blow).

Always communicate with respect and try to put yourself on his side. They are also human and are doing their best to officiate the game as professionally as possible.

Parker the Role Model

A role model is defined as 'a person whose behaviour, example, or success is or can be emulated by others, especially by younger players.' Athletes, gang leaders and celebrities comprise most of the role models in our communities in today's society.

I have spoken to Bernard Parker's peers, friends, well-known personalities in soccer, opponents, coaches, colleagues, supporters, and upcoming soccer players and everyone agrees that Parker is a real symbol of a role model.

Parker said that he always uses himself as a reference when he speaks to school children and aspiring soccer players by telling them about his struggling upbringing raised by a single mom and sometimes having no food to eat. 'That didn't stop me from dreaming or lead me to give up.'

Growing up in a community known for gangsterism and drug abuse inspired him more to become someone, rather than end up as a statistic. 'I was not born a superstar, but I worked hard for what I have and have become. So, everyone can become what they desire and dream to become.'

Cristiano Ronaldo is often misrepresented as a superstar. To me, he is a great role model, and a lot of youngsters are looking up to him. I am one of his biggest fans and supporters. My wish is to meet him one day. After the late Pele, he is one of the best footballers on this planet, not forgetting our own Benni McCarthy. Unfortunately, people perceive both Ronaldo's and Benni's self-confidence as arrogance. They believe in themselves and their talents and abilities and no one can take that away from them. Ronaldo loves himself, which is a good attribute that every person must have.

Players like Ronaldo and Sadio Mane are big givers of note, giving back to disadvantaged communities. I will be establishing the Bernard Parker Foundation to do likewise. I am inspired, motivated and I am going to get involved. I will encourage all our players to do likewise.

CHAPTER 11

SPIRITUAL OWNERS OF THE GAME

Picture Credit Kaizer Chiefs

I enjoyed great support from our supporters and only a few fans harassed me, but I don't have any hard feelings towards anyone. Thank you for your love and support and for helping me grow, match after match.

This letter was written before Parker's contract at Kaizer Chiefs came to an end on 30 June 2022.

Dear Amakhosi Supporters

Firstly, I am very grateful to our loyal and faithful supporters who stood with Kaizer Chiefs through thick and thin. As a club we had some challenging seasons, for a big team that was used to winning trophies it is really hard to comprehend not bringing home a single trophy for the past six years.

The management and players are trying their best to make our team win again and for the glory days to come back again. Covid-19 has also made things worse, and we needed our supporters very badly, especially during the bubble. We missed our supporters. We missed the yellow and black and the '*gees*' (spirit).

I am not making any excuses for our poor performances, but we need our supporters to rally behind us, and as players we understand the significant role that you as supporters play and how you motivate us when the chips are down.

I am writing this open letter to you to plead with you to rally behind the team and management.

Our desires as players have always been to make it the best club in South Africa and conquer Africa. We want to bring the smiles back to your faces again.

I must say that, for the past 11 seasons at Kaizer Chiefs, I gave my everything on and off the field and only wanted the best for the team. As a human being, one makes mistakes and learns from them and moves forward. I serviced the team with distinction and had some good and bad days.

I was sometimes harassed by some of our supporters on the field, and on social media on numerous occasions, and that broke my heart because I love our team and supporters. I ask for forgiveness if I have failed you in a way that I was not aware of.

I apologise for the times that I have disappointed you, but please understand that I always gave my best for our team and our supporters.

I believe that the club is rebuilding and soon will be back to winning trophies again.

Kaizer Chiefs has a very rich history, and you played a huge role as supporters to make it what it is today: successful. Never give up on the team. Our team is nothing without you, our colourful and peace-loving spiritual owners.

Our Chairman, Dr Kaizer Motaung, deserves the best for all his sacrifices in rebuilding Kaizer Chiefs into one of the biggest and most well-run clubs in South Africa and Africa. The Chairman deserves trophies, and we are going to give them to him as players.

Love and Peace
Bernard 'Die Hond' Parker, No 25

This letter was written before the end of my contract with Amakhosi in June 2022. I still love and treasure the yellow and black.

Message from Bra Freddy Saddam Maake

Parker 'Die Hond' 'Ma se kind' listen here: we as supporters, especially me, our hearts are broken. It is sad to see you go. You played for Kaizer Chiefs for 11 years, you gave your heart and your everything to the club. I wish you well for your future and future team.

The team that you are going to join is gaining a star and epitome of professionalism and a great leader.

For other players, it was only a job, but for you, you loved the club, you gave your everything, body soul and spirit. You created goals for other players with no jealousy in your heart. You scored important goals that brought trophies to the team. You cried when others won, and you cried when the team was losing. You were sad and happy on and off the field if the team was not doing well.

Those are signs of a real warrior and someone who defended Kaizer Chiefs with his whole life on the pitch. You served Kaizer Chiefs with love and excellence.

I really thought that the team would keep you as part of the technical staff. You, Itumeleng Khune and Willard Katsande are real legends of the team.

I was saying to other people that they can release everyone, but Parker and Khune saved us a lot in the past. You even scored a beautiful last goal against Swallows to save us from defeat. You are the son of the soil. You are the best from the rest. Keep well and be strong. Don't panic; you will be back soon.

Freddy Saddam Maake
Famous Kaizer Chiefs Supporter and the inventor of the popular stadium buddy the vuvuzela

Mr Vina Maphosa

I arrived at Kaizer Chiefs in July 2012. At the time when Bernard Parker ended his playing career of 11 years at Kaizer Chiefs, I was touching my 10th-anniversary milestone in the employment of the Club.

So, when I arrived at the Club, the narrative was that the Club was in desperate need to turn its fortunes around after the uncharacteristic dry spell from the previous season of 2011/12.

I arrived in the winds of change and Parker was there already from the previous season. I arrived at the same time as the then-new signees of Erick Mathoho and Morgan Gould. The other players like Tsepo Masilela joined in the process of change. These were big names at the time. Mathoho, as a towering, lanky defender, was a big signing from Bloemfontein Celtic. In this era were the likes of Siphiwe Shabalala and Reneilwe Letsholanyane. Who can forget that era of Itumeleng Khune and Tefo Mashamaite? Then there was the MALEMA era that Parker played alongside. MALEMA was a combo of Mandla Masango, George Lebese and George Maluleka.

With Parker, we clicked from the word go. We started talking outside official chats about family matters. He took a keen interest in my family and naturally I reciprocated by checking on his well-being all the time. Memory lane fast-tracked to the performances on the pitch. I had a disappointing debut match as a club official. Mamelodi Sundowns hammered us by 4–1 in the 2012 MTN8. It was my first official match for the Club, as it was for several other new players and coach Stuart Baxter as well.

The following week, we went to play away against AmaZulu in a Premiership match. Parker banged in four goals in the 6–0 drubbing of Usuthu at Durban's Moses Mabhida Stadium. I will never forget that match, coupled with Parker's performance. He was a marvel to watch, and I still have vivid images of his celebration with the rising hands and peace sign in the air. 'Die Hond' was on fire. This victory signalled the season of glory for Amakhosi. Chiefs went on to win the league and Nedbank Cup double. Remarkably, many will remember that Parker capped that season with a winning goal in the extra against a gallant SuperSport United, to lift the Nedbank Cup, the venue was a full Moses Mabhida Stadium.

In the same successful era, we went on to celebrate a league and MTN8 Cup double a season later, again Parker playing a key role during that triumphant season.

On the sidelines was working with him in the roadshows and other club activations. With Parker, we always touched on matters of the future. The plans, his ambitions, and his love for coaching as a career. I remember when he registered to study for a marketing diploma. He was excited throughout the learning process until he achieved the qualification and graduated. Mostly our engagement has been brotherly and occasionally I took up the role of father figure, given our biological age differences. The sound of Bra

Vina, from an acclaimed sports star, will stay with me forever. I wish him well.

Parker, to me, epitomises a genuine hardcore and consummate professional. He conducts himself appropriately and was never reluctant to take up front-row seats even on impromptu or last-minute assignments. He played a significant and exemplary role by leading the troops, even when the chips were down towards the end of his playing career.

Punctuality is one of his strengths. With Parker as a media officer, you never panic when you have a scheduled appearance or interview with him. Always neatly dressed, typical appearance of what is a hallmark of a tradition that the forefathers of Kaizer Chiefs started back in the day, afros, bell bottoms and were affectionately known as the Glamour Boys.

In bidding him farewell, I recall his role during the season when Chiefs reached the 2021 CAF Champions League final. Parker played a starring and leading role as the captain of the team. He scored a massive goal, a beautiful header, to give Chiefs 1–0 in the group stages against a much-fancied Wydad Casablanca.

I wish 'Die Hond' all the best in his next moves. I am confident he will continue to be a shining star in whatever he does going forward.

Mr Vina Maphosa
Corporate Communications Manager
Kaizer Chiefs

CHAPTER 12

DR KAIZER MOTAUNG, CHAIRMAN OF KAIZER CHIEFS

My desire as a child was always to play for Kaizer Chiefs and to meet the legendary Dr Kaizer Motaung, whom my mother and other older people admired so much.

He came up with the name of the football club by joining his name with that of his former team, the Atlanta Chiefs. Dr Motaung is not an ordinary man but an institution. I always dedicated some of my Man of the Match awards to the club's chairman, Dr Kaizer Motaung. We must respect the badge and the architect of Kaizer Chiefs, Dr Kaizer Motaung. We need to keep the slogan alive as players wherever we go: 'Love and Peace'.

Kaizer Chiefs was formed by a great visionary leader, someone I regard as a great role model and a father figure in my life. He sacrificed so much for this beautiful game, and he took care over the years for so many players and their families. He created so much employment and created a lot of soccer stars and millionaires out of soccer players who came from previously disadvantaged communities by giving us the opportunity to play for Kaizer Chiefs and display our God-given talents.

It is remarkable how he loved and cared about his supporters, and it pained him if we didn't bring in any trophies to make them happy. He regards their unconditional love and undying support through the years since the formation of Kaizer Chiefs as the lifeline of the team very highly.

I honour and respect the University of Cape Town (UCT) for honouring Dr Kaizer Motaung. UCT, one of the world's leading tertiary institutions, bestowed the title of Doctor of Social Science Honoris Causa upon Chiefs' Chairman. Well-deserved and long overdue.

For the past 11 years, I have looked up to him as a father. I am what I am as a man because of men like Dr Kaizer Motaung. The influence he has had on my life has helped shape me into the man and father I am today.

I always wanted to repay him back by scoring goals and winning trophies for him. This man sacrificed everything in his life to build a team like Kaizer Chiefs.

This here goes out to you, Dr Motaung. Thank you so much for giving me the opportunity to represent this big club for 11 years. I honour, value and respect you. Love and Peace.

Bernard 'Die Hond' Parker (25)

CHAPTER 13

CRIME, GANGSTERISM, DRUGS, BULLYING AND GBV

*I had to navigate through
poverty, drugs, and violence.*

PARKER

I grew up in a coloured township called Reiger Park. This is in Boksburg, Ekurhuleni. I was blessed to have a schoolteacher, Mr Denzel Bezuidenhout, who believed in me, and who invested his time and love into my soccer career. I honour and respect him for taking me to the School of Excellence for soccer trials – and the rest is history! Sadly, not many youngsters in our townships have a person like Mr Bezuidenhout making such an effort to help them achieve their dreams.

Reiger Park is an environment in which crime, gangsterism and drugs flourish, and if there isn't a strong family structure with a father figure or other mentor to help you keep strong, young people come under a lot of pressure to follow the township norms. I grew up in a one-room shack with only my mother and my brother, and things were hard for us.

It is a shame that our first role models were drug lords and gangsters. Because they can afford the best cars and the most desirable girls, young people want to be like them. It seems to them that gangsterism pays, and they think it is cool to be part of a gang. Crime, alcoholism, drug use and gang culture are huge challenges in our communities. Unrealistic dreams are pedalled to the youth, and the gifts and talents of young people are often destroyed. Poverty and unemployment underlie many of the social ills and life in these communities is very tough and very challenging.

Perhaps, if there were more youth development and educational programmes in the townships, change could be brought about and the youth could be given something more positive to aspire to. Our youth needs to be kept busy with positive activities in our communities. Incentivise them to clean our streets, parks and gravesides.

I still remember when my mother was retrenched, and we had nothing. I made pap every day, and we ate it without sugar or milk for two weeks – for breakfast, lunch and supper. During that time, we had only water to drink. When I look back on those times and what we went through, I understand what the majority of families in our country are still going through.

If I hadn't gone to the School of Excellence, I could easily have succumbed to these bad influences. Peer pressure is strong, and you are confronted with bad options daily. Your choices are limited and there are few opportunities for employment and for getting out of the poverty trap. But at the School of Excellence, I learned to see things differently as they moulded us into both better footballers and better people.

Why do our youth join gangs and what can be done about it?

Gangs give the youth a sense of belonging. Within a gang, they are looking for the love that they don't get at home, and expect to find protection, respect, money and enjoyment. Often, they are recruited by a friend and feel that this is the only way to survive.

Communities, the church and the government need to strengthen the involvement of families and schools with the youth if they want to counteract the appeal of gangs. Teachers and parents need training so that they can better manage disruptive young people at both home and school.

At school, learners should learn interpersonal skills, and youth recreation facilities need to be established to keep the youth busy with positive programmes after school. Gang awareness training should be provided to school personnel, parents and learners. Young people should be made aware of the negative side of gangsterism, to understand that it is not sustainable and can be damaging to their futures.

Life in a gang: 'You don't know who's gonna die next'- By Tracy Ollerenshaw.

Bullying

I was bullied from a young age because I was very small but very talented, skilful and fast. I was bullied for being different. I used to cry a lot and was always running to my mother when the bigger boys bullied me because they were jealous of me because of my sports talents. I always told myself that I would make it in football, no matter my stature. It hurt a lot but I internalised the pain. I turned the bullying into my daily inspiration that one day is one day, and I am going to be a big soccer star and these bullies will eat a humble pie.

What have I learned from this?

1. Bullies are children crying for help and don't know how to show it or ask for help.
2. They put on brave faces and pretend all is well with them while they are broken inside.
3. Bullying can destroy your self-worth, confidence and self-esteem.
4. Bullies are scared children running away from themselves and possibly their conditions at home.

Remember this!

1. Speak out. Don't be afraid to expose bullies.

2. Don't be afraid to tell your parents, educators and people close to you that you are being bullied by someone.
3. Your value doesn't decrease based on someone's inability to see your worth.
4. Never give up on yourself, discover the greatness in you and find your purpose.

Gender-based violence (GBV)

Gender-based violence (GBV) is a widely known problem that is mainly perpetrated by men and boys who tolerate negative masculine practices.

Let's be clear about GBV: not every man or boy is an abuser or rapist, but every man needs to take a stand against it! This cannot be tolerated in our names.

1. Educate yourself and others about GBV and Violence Against Women and Children.
2. Take a stand against GBV and Violence Against Women and Children.
3. They say, 'Hurt people, hurt people'. If you are a victim, speak out! Don't hide it.
4. If you are affected, speak out!
5. If you have witnessed it, speak out; don't remain silent!
6. Stop making dirty jokes about girls and women!
7. Don't be part of groups that sends naked pictures of girls and women around! Remove yourself from that WhatsApp group.
8. Love and respect yourself.
9. Respect your mother, sister, all women and girls.
10. Be the keeper and protector of your mother and sister, all women and girls!

CHAPTER 14

PARKER'S INFLUENCE ON OTHERS

1. FRIENDS

Bernard Parker: From a young boy to a well-grounded man
Mr Denzil Bezuidenhout, Former Primary School Teacher

The rise of Bernard Parker started at LAKESIDE PRIMARY SCHOOL, where I knew him as Bernard Pennels before his surname changed. Bernard grew up in back rooms in Bluebell Street, Reiger Park.

Bernard was a very good long-distance runner at school and an exceptionally good soccer player. This talent I saw when he played in the school's U/9 soccer team. I was the coach of the U/13s at the time. Bernard and my son Beuron became good friends while playing at the school level. I took Beuron to join Boksburg Football Club to play for their U/10s and, seeing how well Bernard was playing, I decided to take him with me. I had to persuade his parents in this regard because they were not too keen about this. I saw his talent at that young age and believed that, playing in Reiger Park, his talents would go to waste. I fetched Bernard every Tuesday and Thursday for practices at Boksburg Stadium. On Saturdays, Beuron and I went to fetch him for their games, and sometimes after the games he spent the day at our house, and I took him home in the late afternoon.

Whilst playing for Boksburg's U/10s, they made the Easterns U/10 provincial team. Bernard was a rare talent who could play any position. His favourite position was striker, as he loved to score goals. I can still remember when they were U/11, Boksburg vs Alberton, how the coach made him goalkeeper after Bernard dribbled Alberton's whole team and scored. My brother-in-law still talks about that day when Alberton was beaten 11–0. His son was playing for Alberton. Bernard made the Easterns first-team age groups from U/10 to U/12 level.

At the U/12 level during that year's provincial tournament in 1999, Bernard was spotted by the scouts of the School of Excellence and there he completed his school career and fine-tuned his soccer skills.

Bernard still used to visit us when he was on holiday during their break at the School of Excellence. There he went through all the age group levels until he was done with school and started his professional career.

He started his career at Thanda Royal Zulu in 2004 and played there until 2009. He left and went and played overseas at Red Star Belgrade. From there he went and played in the Ere divisie in the Netherlands at FC TWENTE from 2009 until 2011, where I believe he did quite well before he returned to South Africa. He came and visited me one Saturday with the offer from Kaizer Chiefs and asked me what I thought and if he should take it. As a Chiefs supporter, I saw it was a good offer at the time and I said he must take it. Ten years later and he is still playing at Kaizer Chiefs. I believe I gave him sound advice.

His debut for Bafana Bafana was in 2007 and he played for our national team until 2015. He made 73 appearances and scored around 23 goals for our country. If my memory serves me well, he is the fourth-highest goal-scorer for South Africa. I still remember, in 2010, when they were preparing for the Confederations Cup at Wits before the World Cup, I was at the Planetarium with our school and the children came and told me that Bafana Bafana was practising there and asked if they could go and watch. I immediately said yes because I wanted to introduce them to Bernard. During their practice break, Bernard and Steven Pienaar came over to us and I introduced them to our kids. That made their day. They could not believe that I knew Bafana players and I explained to them how I knew Bernard.

I see Bernard as a well-grounded young man who has done quite a lot for the community of Reiger Park. I am really proud of him because he listened to me when I told him that when he makes a lot of money he must first, before doing anything else, buy his mom a house, which he did. He also came with beautiful his and hers Fossil watches for me and my wife, just to say thank you. That watch is one of my treasures.

I did not expect anything from him. I am just glad God gave me the wisdom to see the talent and I was able to make a difference in this young man's life.

How different might his life have been if I had not taken him with me to Boksburg Football Club? All the best to Bernard for whatever he wishes to do after he retires from football. My wish is that he will go on to football coaching and also unearth a talent like him in Reiger Park.

Well wishes, Bernard.

Mr Percy Mahlangu

I met Bernard over 15 years ago during his under-23 and Thanda Royal Zulu days. Our friendship grew from strength to strength from there till this day.

I attended a lot of his matches for under-23, Bafana Bafana, and club football, as well as with Thanda Royal Zulu before he moved overseas. He came back from overseas as a complete athlete, very disciplined and reliable. I can say that he is an incredible friend to me and very supportive as well.

I wish him all the best in his future plans, be it in business or talent identification. I do not doubt his abilities. He is a natural-born winner and a natural leader.

Mr David Foster

My best friend Bernard Parker, 'My mooiste Broer', and I run a longstanding family taxi and property rental business. I had the pleasure of sharing a soccer team with Bernard Parker at the junior football level for the Sun United Academy. When I reflect on the early days of our encounter, I saw Bernard as a passionate and talented individual who brought a lot to the game. He was always joking off the field post-training, but on the field, he earned the nickname 'Die Hond' as I remember how swift and quick, he was on the ball on the right and left wings.

We spent most of our youth playing soccer and I later joined another team, Boksburg City, and Bernard progressed to the School of Excellence to build his football career. Later, during our adulthood, in 2018 we established our connection, and naturally we shared the same interests, goals and mindset, which allowed us to grow in our friendship.

In 2020, we established a company called FP Ndawonye Supplies Pty Ltd, which retails tyres, spares, and mechanical, and electrical services. Our fellow brother, Reginald Ayer, later joined us in the same business venture.

I always express gratitude to God for our friendship and keep Bernard, his family, his career and his aspirations in prayer daily. This is the foundation on which our friendship is built: to put our trust fully in God and have faith through positive confession and deed that all things will work out for us at all times.

There is not a day that passes that I do not hear from Bernard and if we don't make contact, it's almost like a void is felt. We speak for over 30 minutes on the phone every day and discuss God, family, life, goals, business and our next moves to achieve greater success. We, fortunately, live in the same area and reach out to each other during the week, and I always feel excited to see him and be greeted by his affectionate smile at my gate. We have braais during the week, do business networking, and always share ideas of where we should take our families for the next holiday or event.

Bernard has become part of my family's life and there is nothing I do or plan without mentioning him and his family. Wendy Parker and my wife share a very good relationship and she often visits us without Bernard, especially when he is away. We laugh and get her to speak Afrikaans and always try to catch up on family life.

Our kids love online games, and they can play forever and when Bernard or I walk into our son's rooms we send a greeting to each other's household through our boys as they enjoy their games. Bernard has become the person in my life who is an inherent part of a bright future we will share through God's grace.

At the moment, we have set ourselves a six-month goal to achieve our business goals and have put the necessary plans in place to ensure we remain focused and dedicated to achieving this. I always look forward to his calls before and after training and this completes my day. The good is always having long chats over the phone, and when we meet, we share laughter about the highlights of the week or month. We always try to take the positive away from whatever is going on around us in the country and bring it home as a lesson to become better fathers, husbands, and friends.

If the business is not making sales and our conversations become difficult, we quickly discuss and implement strategies to turn things around. Last night, we had a family memorial and immediately after Bernard called, I walked out of the meeting to take his call, and this has become something special for me, knowing we often call each other despite our hectic schedules. When we chat it's almost like we are meeting for the first time as we catch up on almost anything and each time get to know each other better. I remember during Gavin Hunt's era; he raised several challenges at work and often visited after training. We always seemed to have the right words at the right time for each other, especially when I experienced difficulty with our family business. We are ready to take on the next challenge following each of our interactions.

Bernard is a unique, person filled with great talent. He has a good heart and his focus on life has earned him great success. He is always looking for ways to achieve more and his calm spirit and mental strength set him apart from the rest.

I see Bernard as a promising family steward, successful entrepreneur, football coach and mentor to our youth and adults alike. I always admire how he manages to lead a balanced life, despite facing obstacles within his football career. I always remind him about his biography and establishing an academy in Reiger Park as a symbol of hope and success for the next generation. I am always looking forward to his success and shared a word with him two months ago that whatever he touches will prosper in this life.

He is truly an inspiration and blessing to many. This is evident during our trips to Warmbaths, where I always try to protect him from the paparazzi, but he remains calm and is always his true self. His heart for people is often seen in interactions with his fans and wherever we go we always get confronted by people asking for a picture and sharing a greeting.

Our conversation always ends with 'Love You Broer' and I would like to end this letter on the same note. I will see you for now, as I have a bible college assignment due today.

Love You, Broer!

Mr Jerome 'Slim' du Plooy

My name is Jerome du Plooy, also known as Slim Parker. I am an entertainer and media personality specialising in radio, TV (actor and presenter) international emcee, motivational speaker and philanthropist.

I'd like to scratch the word friendship (laughs) because he's my big brother (serious face), but on the real, that's my big brother. There's some quote I read as a kid but could never understand until I met my big brother in this life, and it goes as follows:

'Not all brothers are blood-related. A brother not born of blood can still be a brother in every other way.'

This is true, man. James Buys, one of Bernard's close friends, always sums it up best by saying I'm his baby brother. My late mother was never selfish in sharing me, and I thank her for that because I'm from a small family. I grew up in a household where my mother was a helper and till today, I'm treated like a son and brother in that home and it made me realise that family is not always blood.

There are many examples of that, but I always say the perfect example is me and Bernard. With that said, Hond is my ride-or-die, my role model and my inspiration! We are super close and as he always says, I'm the closest person to him and he's the closest person to me. The big me, as I always say. But most of all he's my twin soul and vice versa. We always joke that he's the big me and I'm the small him (laughs). His parents are like my own and Jas is my big brother also, the same way my mom loved Bernard when she was still here. He promised her before she passed that he would always have my back and look out for and after me, which he has done till this day.

The crazy thing is that, after I got back from an NBA gig in Toronto in 2016 where I emceed during All-Star weekend, I think she waited for me to get back. A couple of weeks after that she passed and to me it was like saying she's leaving me in the hands of Bernard because she knew I'd be safe. I love Bernard to the death of me and he knows that I'll always be there for him, the way a little brother is supposed to be.

It's crazy, since 2015... but let me tell you this beautiful story. A mutual friend and teammate of Bernard, Morgan Gould, to whom I am forever grateful also, as I always say made me and Bernard realise we are brothers. He knew I was looking for a big brother, the same way Bernard was looking for a little brother. He told Bernard my story and how I grew up, which was quite similar to Hond, and I think it touched him, which then made him want to meet me.

We met at the village. I'll never forget; Morgan drove me there and said he had a surprise. When we drove up Lena Road, there stood my icon. I've never jumped out of a car so fast in my life. We spoke for a bit, he gave me his number, and then we followed each other on Instagram. At this point my eyes fill up with tears coz I'm this kid looking at this guy I admire. He goes to the back of his Jeep, pulls out a jersey tailor-made for me, hugs me, looks at Morgan and says this is my Laaitie now, hugs me again and mentions I'm his little brother. He promised me he'd see me soon, which was at his favourite artist Rick Ross's show in Durban. That's where we bonded more, spoke for a bit, took a selfie and the rest is history.

Dope boys, as Hond would call it.

The joy, good and bad days of your friendship.
The joy is being Bernard's little brother man and him my big bro. I'm kind of like his best friend (laughs) but I'd rather not say that (laughs again). But seriously, being a little brother to one of the world's most valuable football players is great. We are very close, tight-knit. Also, the joy comes from the games we (Chiefs) would win because we would analyse everything over the phone performance and all of that. It's also a joy when we achieve things, like awards, or me getting an acting gig; the dreams and visions we have and seeing some of them come to life; the celebration of birthdays because we are living in an era where we are not sure what tomorrow holds, so just also appreciating every moment, every phone call and all the little things, man.

Good days are about the small wins (like day-to-day accomplishments, what we are striving to achieve, and all the simple things), talking about my nephews, family, and so on, and just constantly wanting to see each other win. Bad days? Yoh, I don't like those, and they are not many but when they happen, ha (laughs) it's crazy. B scolds me if I slip up and be hard on me, like a big brother should be. I'll get emotional about it, but later on he will explain why he did that, and I'll understand, and it will just make the bond stronger.

Also, the worst is when Chiefs lost games. It would be tough, he'd go silent for a day or two, but I would understand. He'd feel like he let me down because I get so emotional after a game and sometimes, I feel like, after we lost, he maybe thinks he disappointed us (me, the family, fans, team, and himself) but it's not always the case. It's just all part of the game.

Everything that he is and stands for! His heart! His love for people! His selflessness and just the ultimate humble human being he is. He is there for everybody and makes sure that everyone is good and okay. He loves to see people happy and winning in this life. He will even take of his last to assist the next person. Every day I pray that God blesses him abundantly for what he does. I don't think there are that many more people left on this earth with a golden heart like that. He is always there to offer advice and motivate, but he ultimately wants to see everyone in his life win and accomplish things.

Where do you see him in the next three years and why?
Being a successful businessman (it's already started but I see him owning more established businesses in various fields because of the leader he is).

Travelling the world with family. He speaks about that a lot, so I pray he finds time to make that happen. He's constantly so busy (laughs), so that's one of the things I hope he does in the next three years. Being the great family man that he is, family is everything to him.

Also, becoming a coach at Kaizer Chiefs or even nationally. He loves the game a lot and has so much knowledge to offer the next generation who will take the game forward.

Hopefully a motivational speaker as well as a soccer analyst for major networks.

Implementing successful school programmes around the country and bettering the young. I know that's one of his passions. Also, him just living life and enjoying God's blessings and every moment.

Mr Emmanuel Kunene

My friendship with Bernard Parker (though I am used to calling him D-Hond!!). Well, I will keep it formal.

Hmm, my friendship with Bernard Parker. I can say words that will mount up to novels, but all I can say is, it's a friendship that has been watered with trust, joy, kindness, reliability, loyalty, respect, disagreements and agreements that made us friends/brothers. I have known him for eight years now. We came across each other in Boksburg.

I was still practising motor mechanics as one of my big brother's workers. He had gotten stuck with a tyre puncture on his vehicle, and he was looking for a wheel spanner, I helped him without knowing he was a soccer player (haha), and when he had to pay I said no, it's okay brother.

With Parker being a good-hearted man, he came back again to the shop to support us and at times would chill while the car was being serviced. From there a friendship was created. Great moments happened while going out together as boys and family lunch invitations ... just as human beings. And sad moments will always be there. Some of the sad moments were the times when they would lose a match (lol, D-Hond would be kind of cold), but I would understand. You know us men and sports.

And one other sad moment was when he lost his father. (We all know death is never a friend.) May his father rest in peace.

What makes Bernard special? To me, it's not his great soccer skills or form. No, no, no! To me, it's his humbleness, consideration and respectful personality. This man is very humble. Believe me, anyone who has ever come across Parker will tell you the same!

Where I see him in the next three years? If not still playing, surely, he will be one of the sports analysts as well as a businessman. Besides soccer, he has a creative business mind, although that's always shocking and surprising. Bernard Parker is a man of so many talents; it goes beyond the soccer field. He is a great husband and father to his two sons, something that is lacking among most sportspeople.

Mr Reginald Ayer

My name is Reginald Ayer, and I have been a close friend of Bernard for many years. We come from the same community in Reiger Park and had similar interests in football growing up in Reiger Park. I remember as youngsters, we used to play football every Saturday at the football grounds for our respective clubs as kids. Afterwards, we would all go to the takeaway shops and compromise on a good meal.

It was then that Bernard's talent was really discovered, and he excelled to move to greater heights.

He parted from many of us because he was the one who stood out, he had the talent, and he has not looked back ever since. We came back to meet as friends in our more mature ages and it was about seven years ago when we united again and started hanging out much more and expressing our life as friends.

One thing that Bernard and I have made sure of is to encourage each other as often as possible and to be there to motivate when we go through our rough patches, whether it is work, relationships, or anything that is discouraging for one of us at that point. But most of all we appreciate each other's loyalty which is a big thing for us coming from a community where not everyone turns out to make it.

I see Bernard as a football coach or having some kind of involvement in football in the next three years because he has given so much of his energy with such a passion for the game and has grown with experience and giving it back to the future stars will be in his mind for sure.

The good days of our friendship are always hanging out after a positive week of work from my side or a positive result playing a match from Bernard's side and having a braai with our families, laughing, joking and encouraging each other. I must say we haven't had bad moments as friends because we have a good level of transparency and that is what makes Bernard a special friend to me. He is one of the most humble people I've come across and his work ethic towards success is very inspiring to me. That's why these points have made me appreciate and respect my friends a lot.

Mr Evert Jan, Family friend based Enschede, Netherlands

I met Bernard for the first time somewhere in 2009 when he signed a contract in Belgium. I wanted to meet him because we'd adopted two children from South Africa, and we have a good connection with South Africa, not only because of the two children we adopted but also because we made good friends with people in South Africa who later became like family to us.

The Parker family is like our blood family. We still keep in contact with them since 2009 and we regularly visit one another. Bernard is a very good person, a role model for young football players but also for how he relates to ordinary people. He will not show you that he is this famous person. He is down to earth and humble.

He does not misuse his status and fame for personal use but will uplift a lot of underprivileged people. He is a real family man and loves his wife and children dearly, and even the larger family. He can be used as a real role model to the youth and younger generation, showing them how not to focus on their poor living conditions but to rise above all and become somebody like him.

I think he deserves to be honoured more by South Africans and I hope this book will be supported. I know that a lot of people will be inspired by this book when they read about all Bernard's challenges growing up, challenges on the football field, and personally. I wish him good luck with his book, and I believe that he is going to inspire a lot of youngsters and people to reach for the stars and make the best of their lives here on Earth.

Charley Pietersen

2. PREMIER SOCCER LEAGUE PLAYERS & PERSONALITIES

Mr Lyle Lekay

Teams played for; SuperSport Utd, FC Cape Town, and Bloem. Celtic, Cape Town City, Mamelodi Sundowns and Cape Town City

He's a true professional. I think his career speaks for itself. When Parker played overseas in the Champions League, I remember I was watching Tottenham play the Champions League game against FC Twente and I went to watch the game while I was on trials at Tottenham in London.

He is a true professional and still playing the game at his age. He is Kaizer Chiefs' top goal scorer. I don't know him personally but on the field of play, he is a top professional and he always leads by example.

Mr Vuyo Mere

Teams played for; Hellenic FC, Mamelodi Sundowns, Platinum Stars, Cape Umoya Utd, Bidvest Wits FC, Swallows FC, and TS Galaxy.

I first saw Bernard playing at Benoni United, playing with the likes of Katlego Loke, Tshepo Mashishi, Tshepo Masilela, Mara May and the list goes on. For the mere fact that Bernie could have a space with that quality of a player speaks volumes about his qualities. Looking back, what he has achieved was not a fluke, as he is a hard and dedicated worker. He plied his trade overseas and represented the country on many occasions with distinction.

I was lucky to share the same dressing room with him whilst playing for the national team once. He is still doing well, leading Kaizer Chiefs under difficult circumstances, with the team not doing so well in recent seasons, but he has remained consistent and shown a lot of leadership qualities.

South Africa is super blessed to have Berny as our own because he is a true legend and ambassador of the game. I wish him everything of the best as he continues to do so well in his team.

Mr Siphiwe Tshabalala

Teams played for: Free State Stars, Kaizer Chiefs, Bafana Bafana, Büyüksehir Belediye Erzurumspor, Amazulu.

If my memory serves me well, I played against Bernard in 2006 in the First Division. I was playing for Free State Stars and he was playing for Benoni Premier United and then we later became opponents in the Premier Soccer League when he played for Thanda Royal Zulu. He is a great player, prolific striker and hard worker, and his hard work rewarded him with a move abroad, where he did very well.

I got the opportunity to not only play with him in our national team, Bafana Bafana, but I shared a room with him and that's when I got to know the other side of Bernard: the humble God-fearing man, someone who loves his family. For someone coming from a poverty-stricken area, Reiger Park, known for its crime, drugs and gangsterism, he did very well for himself. He made it through with hard work, resilience and determination. He is someone who advocates for social change in the underprivileged areas and on the field. He is a very hardworking person who hates losing, and who gives us his all, even on a bad day. Bernard would still give his all and one thing you cannot question about him is his commitment and loyalty. He always brought his positivity and energy to training and the field of play, all the time.

We eventually became teammates at Kaizer Chiefs, where we brought success to the club. It breaks his heart when the team is not doing well in terms of winning trophies, and he would always encourage the squad not to give up fighting for the club, supporters, and management. I am fortunate to be part of the team that, together with Bernard, brought some success to the club. We were a bunch of winners. I just want to congratulate 'Die Hond', as he is known on the soccer field as a respectful, humble, and dedicated player.

My man, you deserve all accolades. You've earned them, and you still have a role to play after your playing career is over. You're a man of integrity. You're a prayer warrior, you know, resilient, and you did not get things easily. You know that you work hard for what you want, and you continue being a leader both on and off the field, and I'm sure somewhere there are upcoming players who want to see themselves as the next Bernard Parker. They see themselves in the mirror as the next you. Please keep on going forward. That is a great accolade for a new generation of players who want to be like you. It is an indication of how big you are – that's how great you are – and you are the role model who inspires others to be as selfless and courageous as you are. I am not saying this to please you.

All I can say to our youth is never give up dreaming, always dream big and don't be defined by your poor upbringing and background. Bernard and I are proof and living testimony to that.

My brother, all the best to you and your family and keep going. 'Varavara'. God bless.

Lawrence Siphiwe Tshabalala: In the opening match of the 2010 World Cup, Bafana Bafana midfielder put hosts South Africa 1–0 against Mexico with a terrific strike with his left foot.

Mr Willard Katsande

Teams played for; Feruka, Highway, Gunners, Ajax Cape Town, Chiefs, currently at Sekhukhune United FC.

The first time I met Bernard Parker was when he joined Kaizer Chiefs coming from the European Champions League. I met someone with a good heart and a love of helping people especially young players joining Kaizer Chiefs to settle. It is remarkable and unbelievable for him to be where he is today. It's not by fluke or by chance or luck. It is by hard work, focus and dedication.

He used to cry when the team was not doing well and I can remember when, us being the only two senior players on the field, I would look after the defensive part and he would look after the offensive part, and then I would ask him, what do you think we can do differently when things are really tough? We would work out a plan and communicate it to the rest of the team.

Parker was so dedicated that he sometimes played with an injury, sometimes he played with a sore hamstring, sometimes played with a niggle, sometimes flu, sometimes headaches, sometimes he was in pain, and he still went and was still running more than the youngsters. But overall, he is a guy who puts everyone first. I never saw him angry; he was always happy. There was a time when everyone was attacking us, including the media when things didn't go well with the team. We never responded. We always looked after each other, speaking like, you know what, let's keep going as long as the team does well the rest is okay because we are the guys who've been abused left right and centre when the team doesn't do well, but when the team does well others will get the credit.

After 11 years, I will understand him when he's talking and exactly where he's coming from and exactly what he's trying to say and even now we are still in touch because we're brothers. I mean, football is his Midwest family. We are brothers so we always stay up to date with each other so, yeah. But I think he's overall a great guy. He's a family man, he's a family orientated guy, so that's why he's been in the game for so long, because he's always devoted to his family but overall the guy just loves the game. The guy is always wanting to contribute towards the club's success. When you have somebody like that in your team, your squad, who puts the others ahead of everything, it makes you a huge team. So for me, I don't have any negative things to say about Parker because I've seen him from day one, till my last day with the same club. With Parker I don't see anything negative about him; the guy is positive.

Parker in general is a very positive and energetic person. You can see it in the way he celebrates when somebody else scores a goal, he shows passion and appreciation for the success of others in the team. He is someone who put the interests of the team first. Parker, my friend, thank you for your love and support towards me. I will never forget you.

Mr Siyabonga Nkosi

Teams played for: Bloemfontein Celtic, Kaizer Chiefs, Orlando Pirates, Lamontville Golden Arrow FC, Arminia Bielefeld, Maccabi Netanya, and Supersport United.

Bernard is a very good friend of mine. In fact, he is one of my best friends and is like a brother to me in many ways. We have a very good relationship off the playing field. Apart from playing together at Kaizer Chiefs, we formed a very good understanding even on the field of play because the brotherhood that we have. Football starts there; it starts from a willingness to partner with someone on the field of play. When you're open to that completely, without any reservations, then combinations are fruitful in most cases. I think that was the type of situation that we had between me and him and when we played together.

I personally thoroughly enjoyed it. I was always happy having him next to me in the field of play. I admire the quality that he had. I admire the passion that he had, the character that is about. He is a fighter who never stopped and never quits. He is mentally very strong and his attitude towards his game is just phenomenal. I think a lot of people can learn from that and a lot of youngsters can learn from that, and the technical ability he possesses.

It's unfortunate that he has been underrated in South Africa with that kind of quality. I don't see many people with the type of quality that he has. He shows that quality now and then and for me it's never in doubt because I saw it in close proximity for a long time. He is overall a fantastic player: very intelligent, technically gifted and unselfish. He is a great person on and off the field: a beautiful heart, caring, passionate, thoughtful, and intelligent. He has all the attributes a person needs to form a solid human being. That is one thing that someone like me, who is older than him, can learn from him in terms of life in general. He is a brother who is of high value to me in many ways and I know that his family values are solid, and his other friends can attest to that. He is a phenomenal human being.

Mr Daniel Matsau

Teams played for: Kaizer Chiefs, Bloemfontein Celtic, Hellenic, SuperSport United, Moroka Swallows, Black Aces, and City Pillars striker.

There is so much to say about Bernard Parker. He loves Kaizer Chiefs with his whole heart. You can see in the way he plays for Chiefs: he plays with his heart, body and soul every match.

He is all over the pitch like a 16-year-old player. He plays his heart out. Bernard is a passionate, disciplined and dedicated player who gives his all for the game of soccer and Kaizer Chiefs. He loves what he is doing. That makes him perform at a high level despite his age. His big heart and love for the game make things very easy for him on the field of play. If you love what you are doing, all things fall into place.

He is sometimes treated very badly by our supporters, which I believe is unfair towards him as a person. I wish him all of the best in his future endeavours.

On 27 May 2000, Matsau fired home an 87th-minute goal for a star-studded South Africa under-23 team against New Zealand that sent South Africa to the 2000 Sydney Olympics.

Mr Itumeleng Issac Khune

Top goalkeeper for Kaizer Chiefs and the South African national team. (Bafana Bafana)

I've known 'Die Hond' from the SA U/23 national team that was preparing for the Olympics. He's such a great gentleman and role model on and off the field to so many young lads.

He's a Kaizer Chiefs legend, who is famous for wearing jersey **#25**, a goal-scoring machine, and of course, his iconic celebration where he rubs his shoulder.

Ma se kind, you'll forever be remembered for your positive contribution to South African football. It has been my greatest pleasure sharing the locker room and the field with you.

May the good Lord continue to protect and bless you and the Parkers.

-ITUKHUNE32

Mr Abel 'Chacklas' Shongwe

Teams played for: Mbabane Highlanders FC, Kaizer Chiefs FC, Wits University FC, Dynamos FC, Swallows FC, Pretoria City FC, AmaZulu FC, and Lamontville Golden Arrow FC.

What do I say about this big 'icon'? I'm privileged to get this platform to say one or two things about this great living legend of Kaizer Chiefs. Yes, I have known Bernard for quite some time now. I knew him when he was still with

Thanda Royal Zulu and he went overseas to further his career. He did very well and played in the Champions League with FC Twente. He later came back to join Kaizer Chiefs and that's when we started getting closer.

What I like about Bernard is that he's the kind of player who goes all out and shows his experience and love for the game. You wouldn't know which foot he was going to use, his left or right. I also used both legs and they didn't understand me, and Bernard was really following in my steps whereby you wouldn't know which foot he is going to use. He is a visionary leader and I like the way he is doing things. And the boy is so humble.

In many ways, Kaizer Chiefs are the way they are today because of Bernard. He's been so loyal to the team, a true captain, a humble and hardworking player. We are like family, too. I'm very close to Bernard; he's very close to my heart. I like the way he's humbling himself; I like the way also whenever he's been given a chance to play, he will go all out at his age. He doesn't look back. He's the kind of player who, whenever he's been given the chance, will go all out and do his best for Chiefs.

He's a true leader, he's a true captain, and I like his humbleness and respectfulness: they go a long way. Right now, everything that he is doing can be done after football. He must carry on humbling himself, having that attitude of loving another person. Irrespective of whether you're old or young, you must carry on. He's a good man and I love him with all my heart. A lot of players who achieve success have learned from him the way he does things. He's a player who respects his family. He is a player who respects everyone. When he goes outside, he represents himself and represents Kaizer Chiefs and represents his family too.

Bernard, I wish you all the best in life and keep on being humble and God bless you. Thank you.

3. PERSONALITIES ON PARKER

Mr Johan Erickson – Former Thanda Royal Zulu coach and player Agent based in Spain

Parker was the captain of Benoni United when the Swedish consortium came in and Benoni United was moved to Durban to then be called Thanda Royal Zulu. Parker was one of the players who came with them, and even though he was young he was the captain. He was a natural leader, leading by example, working hard in every training session and being very consistent. He was one of the few players who liked to do extra training after training sessions and, as a matter of fact, he went on to go to Europe. He went to Holland and that was much deserved. He had the right mentality to become a professional football player. I don't need to say much about his football, his football speaks for itself.

I think perhaps more interesting would be that the word that comes to my mind when I think about Bernard Parker is humble. He remained humble, even though he became a famous player. Secondly, honesty. He was a very honest player. When I worked with him, he always gave good, honest feedback, so that was good. Thirdly, hardworking, consistent, very professional, charismatic, great personality, a great smile, generous and intelligent. There isn't anything bad that I can think of to say about Bernard. He's a real top-quality player and human being.

Mr Johan Glennmo - Former Chairman and CEO of Thanda Royal Zulu FC

Just before the 2007/2008 season started, I was the chairman and CEO of Thanda Royal Zulu FC and had just purchased the Premiership club Benoni United. During the briefing with my head coach, I was made aware that we had a special talent in the squad. His name was Bernard Parker. I ran the club for two years and Mr Parker was the biggest talent. I wasn't surprised that he made it to Europe, both at Red Star Belgrade and Twente.

But even though he became Dutch champion with Twente and became a national team player, it is not his skills on the pitch that stand out for me. South African soccer is full of players with great skills and technique, who are able to do amazing things with the ball that drives the crowds wild. Mr Parker showed his skills early on the field with a great understanding of the game and had the skills to become a crowd favourite, but what made Mr Parker stand out from the other skilled players was that his technique was also functional. He was always able to make sure that his actions on the field helped his team achieve its goals.

I have a lot of great memories of Mr Parker from this time, but there are two episodes that stand out for me.

The first is from October 2008, when I arranged for Mr Parker and his teammate Felix Obada to travel to Malmö, Sweden, for trials with Malmö FF. They practised with the team and, on finishing the trial, they were selected to play with Malmö FFs under-21 team in the Swedish under-21 championship final against IFK Norrköping. Both teams were allowed to use over-age players and joining Mr Parker and Mr Obada were, among others, Swedish national player Jimmy Durmaz.

During the game, both Mr Parker and Mr Obada played well. Mr Parker, who is just as good with his right foot as with his left, played predominantly with his left during the game. The game ended in a tie and went to penalties. Mr Parker wanted to take a penalty and was selected to take the first. He stepped up and with great confidence put the penalty in the net with his right foot. Hasse Borg, the then sports director of Malmö FF screamed out something like, 'Unbelievable, he plays the whole game with his left foot and scores a great penalty with his right!' This confidence seems to be something that Mr Parker has from his upbringing because it seems to come naturally to him.

It is also prevalent in my next great memory from that time. The team had successfully managed to survive our first season and we were on a preseason camp with the team to prepare for the upcoming 08/09 season. Our head coach, Roger Palmgren, and his assistant Johan Eriksson had, of course, also seen Mr Parker's great talent and the previous season he had been a regular starter. Now Coach Palmgren had called a team meeting in a conference room to set initial directions for the coming season for the team but, before he had a chance to start, Mr Parker wanted to speak to his teammates.

What came next is the greatest proof for me of what leadership skills and maturity Mr Parker possessed at such an early age. Mr Parker stood up for his teammates, most of them older than him and many much older than him and gave a speech stating how proud he was to be their teammate after surviving such challenging obstacles. He went on to say how much he believed in them all and that he was looking forward to a successful season. He believed in his team. He had confidence in his ability and his teammate's ability.

He finished his speech with a question. He asked the question in a very humble way. In a very humble way, but with great confidence. He asked them if he could have the great honour to be their captain. They all said, 'Yes'. Mr Parker's leadership and values off the pitch give me great comfort that Mr Parker has a great future now that he steps off the pitch as a pro player one last time. I wish you all the best in the future!

FC Twente – Mr Richard Peters – Press Officer

On 15 July 2009, FC Twente announced that Bernard Parker would join FC Twente's squad. Bernard was 23 years old at the time and impressed during the Confederations Cup in the game against New Zealand. In that match, he scored two goals. Bernard had previously played six months on loan for Red Star Belgrade. For that club, he scored six goals in 16 games. FC Twente was very happy with his arrival. He was presented by former coach Steve McClaren to the public and the press, along with Bryan Ruiz. Bryan Ruiz and Bernard Parker were the replacements for the departed internationals Eljero Elia and Marko Arnautovic.

Bernard played for one year for FC Twente. That was exactly the year in which FC Twente became champions of the Netherlands for the first time in history. His presence was very important, even if he didn't play all the matches. After winning the championship no one has forgotten how he entered Enschede in an open bus with his teammates. Bernard was wearing a red shawl around his head.

He was a very amiable man and was very much loved by his fellow players.

Although Bernhard left for the Greek league after one year, FC Twente looks back with great pleasure on his presence at the club.

Bernard still shows his commitment to FC Twente. Last winter, FC Twente played the farewell match of Bryan Ruiz in Costa Rica. Parker was one of the first former players who sent a congratulatory message and a word of thanks to Bryan Ruiz.

Coach Stuart Baxter

Former South African National Football team and the Kaizer Chiefs coach. He is currently the manager of Helsingborgs IF in Sweden.

When I first arrived in South Africa. Bernard Parker's professionalism was the first thing that struck me. I didn't feel it was usual, with all due respect, for players playing in the South African league to be so professional. Indeed, I found more of that type of professional player at Kaizer Chiefs.

Bernard is one of those players who always likes to link his knowledge of the game with his abilities and skills for every position he plays. He was one of the first players who approached me when I joined Kaizer Chiefs and who was always eager to learn how to improve his skills. His dedication and eagerness to learn benefited the clubs that he played for as well as his country.

I soon realised that Bernard wasn't only a good professional, and the more I got to know him the more I realised that he was an excellent person both on and off the field; a role model for other players and at the same time a very caring person in the community.

If Bernard Parker ever needed a reference, I would certainly be the first one in line to give him that. Probably one of the greatest compliments I can pay to Bernard is that, while other people were calling for Bernard's demise in professional football, he kicked on and on and on and kept his levels and kept his integrity and proved everybody wrong.

I'm sure that whatever Bernard does in the future, he will bring those same qualities to the fore. I wish him good luck for the future.

Mr Theophilus "Doctor" Doctorson Khumalo - Former Kaizer Chiefs, Ferro Carril Oeste, Columbus Crew & Bafana Bafana Player

This is Coach Doctor Khumalo. I am so privileged and honoured to be asked by Bernard Parker to share a few words and memories about our relationship over the past years.

I have a simple question that I want to ask: is there anyone who has a photo or a video that shows Bernard Parker being angry? I would like to see it, please, because I've never seen him angry. All I know, from what I've seen or witnessed, is that I've seen those white teeth laughing more often than on an angry face. So, if anyone out there has a picture or a video or something that shows Bernard Parker being angry, I would like to see it.

In essence, what I'm trying to say is that the journey we have travelled - myself and Parker - has been tremendous. It was fruitful, unbelievable and a very friendly one. When we talk about a social factor in football, we talk about the on and off social factor. It happened that I have off-the-field experience of Bernard's behaviour and how as a human being he reacts outside football. I think there's nothing different that he does on the field and off the field: his attitude is still the same.

The most significant thing off the field is that he is a friendly boy. He's very easy to approach when spoken to, but I would like to believe that on the field he is a very professional player, very dedicated and probably has a belief like I had when I was still playing. I didn't believe in losing. A loss to me would tear me apart and I saw that in Bernard in some instances when we lost games. Yes, he is a winner. I've never seen him rattling off his teammates or showing some ugly gesture, but what I saw were leadership qualities because in football we don't condone violence whatsoever. Having said that, we are not an institution like a preschool, where we keep kids and make them feel at home in football. It's a man's game.

About Bernard, I must say I was privileged and honoured to have managed him as his coach. I've seen him grow from playing in KZN for Thanda Royal Zulu and then going abroad and then playing for the national team and eventually he came to play for Kaizer Chiefs. I happened to be an assistant coach to some of the coaches who coached him. I must say that personally we had an unbelievable relationship. I would at any given time ask him to give me something in order for us to win the game and all, especially in the Soweto derbies or in cup games, without any disappointment.

I am who I am today because the accolades that I've got are through hard work, the sweat that he puts in on the field and the respect I have for the Kaizer Chiefs supporters are because of him and his colleagues. The sweat and the hardships that they show on the field. I must say again that I am very much humbled and honoured to have coached Bernard.

I wonder how Bernard would fit in if he were playing in my era? I bet you he'd probably be one of the best goal-scorers in the world, not just in South Africa. I'm not taking anything away from his teammates, but it's just that I envy his way of approaching the game. He makes things easy for the midfielders but unfortunately, from where I'm seated. I'm not insinuating anything, and I am not being judgmental of anybody; I'm just saying it would have been a pleasure to have played with Bernard and I believe we would have banged those goals in.

Here is Bernard Parker, who is dedicating this book to all those who will be reading it. I would like to believe this is how he wants to share his journey with everybody interested in learning who and what Bernard Parker is all about.

This is the perfect way for a legend like Bernard Parker to share his knowledge and experience with upcoming youngsters and also to show even older people what it takes for one to be on top. Personally, I've learned some things from Bernard and I always say, irrespective of your position, you need to learn to understand and respect any human being who lives in this world and Bernard is one of those people who has shown that it's not just about him being a public figure – no, one of the best players in the world - but he really cares about those who are about to start to make their dreams come true.

I applaud and compliment Bernard for a sterling job because, for people to remember you, you need to leave behind a legacy. I would like to believe that Bernard is one of the players who is leaving a great legacy in South African football. He has done so much in such a way that each time after scoring a goal he performed his trademark of polishing his elbow at the corner of the field. I've seen in all the tournaments around the country the influence he had on youngsters performing his trademark. He has a great influence on young aspiring footballers. They want to be better players. I just want to say, Bernie, thank you very much for your time, for your respect and for everything that we've done together at Kaizer Chiefs and in the football fraternity.

I would like to wish you all the best of luck in your endeavours. May the almighty God bless you and your family. Believe it or not, there's more that we need out of you in this football fraternity. I strongly believe that you can lend a hand to those who are in need of your experience and your brains.

I just want to thank you also for taking the time to write this book. To share your knowledge with those youngsters from all over South Africa and the world. I just want to wish you all the best, boy. I must say what a great player, what a great personality and humour you have. Once more, anybody out there, if you have a picture or video where Bernard is shown being angry, please send it to me I would really appreciate it. I haven't seen this man angry. I just want to see what he looks like when he is angry. That statement on its own says a lot. Thank you, Bernie, for trusting me, thank you for giving me the opportunity to say a few words in your book. I wish you all the best.

You can call on me at any time and moment when you feel like talking to somebody, I'll always be there for you boy, OK all the best son.

Coach Muhsin Ertugral

Coach Muhsin Ertugral's career in South Africa
1999–2003 Kaizer Chiefs, 2003 Santos, 2006–2007 Ajax Cape Town, 2007–2009 Kaizer Chiefs, 2009 Ajax Cape Town, 2011–2012 Golden Arrows, 2013–2014 Ajax Cape Town, 2015–2016 Mpumalanga Black Aces, 2016 Orlando Pirates, 2017–2018 Ajax Cape Town, 2019 Maritzburg United.

Bernard Parker caught my eye, as I am always looking for young talented players to bring in. At that time, I was with Kaizer Chiefs. I used to go to Durban and watch some games. He was playing for Royal Thanda Zulu. We later played against them, and I talked to Bobby to find out how we could get Bernard Parker to Kaizer Chiefs.

Unfortunately, we were too late, and he had already signed a deal to move to Holland.

He attracted my attention with his quick thinking in difficult circumstances. The intensity of his actions and his precision were what caught my eye. It is very seldom that you see that at his age and he was ranking completely above the rest.

His potential showed when he moved to a league that is very difficult to go to from outside of their youth development.

Later, Bobby went for him and brought him to Chiefs.

Personally, I think he has lots to give through his experience in international football and, hopefully, he will stay in football after his career, to pass his legacy on to the next generation, which really needs role models like him.

Coach Gavin Hunt

Teams Managed
Seven Stars, Hellenic FC, Black Leopards, Moroka Swallows, SuperSport United, Bidvest Wits, Kaizer Chiefs, and Chippa United.

I came across Bernard in September 2020, when I joined Kaizer Chiefs, and the first thing that struck me was his professionalism and his attitude towards the game, which blew me away, and you know that football is about professionalism and attitude. I noticed his commitment and dedication in training, and the way he plays, and he was certainly one of the shining lights at Kaizer Chiefs. I cherished and admired him. I moved him back to play in the middle of the field and he did exceptionally for us.

I have admired him through the years, and I have seen him flourish and blossom as a player from the outside. I then had the opportunity to know him better at Kaizer Chiefs. His moral was very low, and he started to pick up very quickly when I joined the team, and he carried the captain's arm belt with dignity and respect. I'm sure as his years in football are coming to an end he will always excel in other departments, like marketing and coaching, because of his abilities and attitude.

He is a good person and somebody whom I admired as a player, and that's obviously one of the reasons why I felt he should be captain of the club. To become captain of the team obviously changes certain players' personalities and attitudes, and there are more demands and responsibilities. Bernard, I thought you knew the demands of playing up front were not going to be the same as when you were a youngster.

Your experience, skills and knowledge are going to be needed at all times. It is not going to be easy but keep that hunger and love for scoring goals alive and be the best support and assistant for the younger players. You've got a good eye for a goal, and you can still score with both feet.

When I left Kaizer Chiefs, we were in the semi-final of the Champions League, and you know I can't give him enough credit for how he stuck up for me. He'd been with a lot of coaches there. He'd gone through all the good times and bad times, and I could only wish him well and have great admiration for the man and his family. I am quite blessed to have known him and I wish him well in his future endeavours. If more South African players could be like him, we would have a much better game of football in this country and it's just a pity that he is at the wrong end of his career and he is not starting his career, because the game needs people like him.

So, God bless, Bernard. I wish you well, son, and I'm sure we'll see you around in the future.

Mr Z T Hlubi - COO TS Galaxy Football Club

Parker is a legend and is exemplary on and off the game, so it was no brainer for us to make the decision to bring him to TS Galaxy. He has given us more than we expected. He's a leader and is always willing to go over and above his call of duty and he leaves all of himself in the field of play. We are fortunate to have a player like him in our team. We know that his life story will, through this book, motivate the youth and show them what you can achieve through commitment, dedication and discipline.

Mr Michael Abrahamson – Sout Africa's top mentalists, well-known sports commentator and experienced Master of Ceremonies.

I've commentated on Bernard Parker in a number of his matches, both for Chiefs and Bafana Bafana. He is prolific, a very talented striker, and a man with an eye for goal. He has a powerful shot, can make some very good runs into space and is very good on the ball, and is also a good dribbler. He is a man who certainly has a good awareness of the game and can sense opportunities and grab them. Bernard is a terrific footballer to watch. He has been accredited by the clubs he played for and his country. He has a glittering career ahead of him with many good stats to be proud of.

Mr Stanton Frederiks

Teams played for: Wits University, Grasshopper Club Zürich, Kaizer Chiefs, FC Moscow, Orlando Pirates, SuperSport United, Pierikos FC, South Africa U-20, South Africa.

Just like most South African footballers, Bernard Parker has emerged from the bottom of the socio-economic ladder and made it to the top.

His hard work and dedication to his craft are evident in the performances he currently displays late in his career.

For me, his ability to play numerous positions is evidence of the quality he possesses. I've always marvelled at his ability to use both left and right feet equally as venomously! I never played alongside him, but whenever I came into contact with him his respect and humility were evident.

He is an example of 24-hour professional!

All the best with the rest of your career and exciting future beyond...

Mr Jermaine Craig – Former Media Manager 2010 FIFA World Cup Organising Committee South Africa and Global Communications Manager at South African Tourism

Bernard Parker is a model professional, who epitomises the sacrifices it takes to have longevity in a football career. He is, of course, one of the best strikers and finishers South African football has ever produced, but he complemented his talent with the extremely hard work required to be successful.

He is a model professional in his lifestyle off the pitch, his attitude and commitment to training, and his discipline, and he is a model professional for all aspiring footballers. He is the ultimate team man and a proven leader, on and off the pitch.

His long career in Europe and South Africa is a testament to his ability and work ethic, and he deserves his place in the annals of South African footballing history.

Mr Thabiso Tema - South African Award-winning On-Air Personality, Presenter, and sports commentator

'Die Hond' Bernard Parker is another one who will also make sure that his name is written permanently in the history of South African and International football. Certainly, in the PSL Era, Bernard Parker must go down as one of the PSL 'Kings'. I mean, for the longest time, he scored in every season that he has played in the PSL. You know he had a fantastic record as a goal scorer.

He also had a short stint in Europe, and I thought that he would have lasted longer in Europe than he did, but when he did come back – I'm not even fully sure of the circumstances around him coming back to South Africa – he signed for Kaizer Chiefs. He's always been one who respected the game, and he's looked after himself well. That's why it's carried him until now and he's still able to perform at the highest level. He's a leader and gentleman of the game and he leads by example, so he doesn't even have to shout and scream at people. Just by younger players watching him play, they can learn a lot from him.

I think it's just something that we struggle with a lot in this country. We are so quick to write off players when they reach the age of 30 and I'm not sure where it comes from, especially when you think about how late the average South African player comes into the game. We speak about a 24-year-old as a youngster, but the truth is in South Africa it's not. It's not just a football thing, but it's a cultural thing too. I think it's something that has to do with our society in general, especially for black South Africans.

My father died when he was in his thirties. He was already settled at this age, with two children: my sister and me. He had a home, and he was a university graduate. He was a man whose career was on the up. What I'm saying is that he had lived a full life. Even though he died so young, he left a legacy behind. I think with us these days – I mean when you're 24 – you are still a 'laaitie'. When I was 24, I was not even close to being married. Maybe life back then was a little bit tough, and it forced you to mature quickly. With us, we grew up a little bit softer, a little bit pampered. Even with the 'laaities' from the township, they have it easy. They matured later in life. And I'll put that word 'easy' in inverted commas.

What I am saying is that they have everything easy because they have more options, so a lot of these laaities who will drop out of school, it's out of choice, unlike their parents. They are too lazy knuckle down and do their schoolwork, but they think that they can make a life playing football, like Parker, but they don't know his journey and struggles.

We tend to let players go easily when they're over thirty. Kaizer Chiefs, in my opinion, let Bernard Parker go too soon. I think he still had a massive role to play. In fact, if you think about how he played under coach Gavin Hunt, he was Gavin's most important player: he was a man revived. Gavin believes in experience. I think they let him go too soon and you can see also what TS Galaxy is getting out of him. I think the fact that he's played this long – and I'm sure he is going to play a couple more years – is because he's a top-class professional. He has respected the game and as a result the game respects him.

But you can see that also in his choices off the field of play: the fact that he chose to study, and he settled down a while ago and got married. You can see that his wife, Wendy, keeps him on the straight and narrow as well. That is keeping him focused. That focus translates into every element of his life, and I have great admiration for what he has achieved.

He is a fantastic professional, and like I said, the game has been very good to him. He played for Bafana Bafana and internationally. He played on the biggest stages of the world in Europe. I think he can look back on his career with pride. I think he's a credit to the community of Reiger Park, from where he comes, as well. He has always remained very firmly rooted in his community.

I hope that he is admired and has inspired a lot of youngsters from those kinds of areas. Interestingly, Charley, you are writing books about Lucas 'Masterpieces' Moripe and Bernard Parker, both of who are exceptional players, although they played in two different eras.

Bernard will never enjoy the status of players who would have been much more popular with the fans than him because of their fancy play, instead of being workaholics like Bernard. If you look at the body of work, and you look at the numbers, there's no comparison. I'm just trying to think of players who started playing with Bernard and were popular among the fans. They played the flashy stuff, but they are no longer playing, and he is still around.

Bernard doesn't play the kind of football that excite the crowds, and they ignored him, but that didn't stop him. His record speaks for itself. I think that what he has achieved in the game will speak for itself. You don't need to be Mr Popularity, but history will judge him well, and those who know the game and the coaches with whom he's worked will all speak the same way about him. Speak to any journalist about Bernard Parker and I'm sure they will echo my sentiments about the kind of guy he is.

His personality as well: he is a perfect gentleman, soft-spoken, not one to hype himself. He is not a loudmouth. That is why guys like him, who are not big-time Charlies – you know, the ones who always want to be the centre of attraction – tend to be forgotten, but ultimately history will judge them very kindly, long after many of those he played with.

I'm looking forward to reading your story about him. Thank you.

Bernard, remain as humble as you are, my man. Our beautiful game needs legends like you who are and will remain great role models to our youngsters.

Mr Brian Mofokeng - On-Air Personality, Presenter, and sports commentator

I remember first seeing Bernard playing for Thanda Royal Zulu, way back in the day, before he eventually went overseas to play for the likes of FC Twente before returning to be part of Kaizer Chiefs. When he returned, he also set a record for the club, scoring the most goals in the league, which surpassed the record that was previously held by Simphiwe Tshabalala.

We cannot forget the time he had in Bafana colours, where he scored 23 goals. But for me, the best show was between 2013 and 2014 when he contributed around ten goals for Bafana Bafana, during the era of coach

Gordon Igesund. I still believe that, had he stayed longer and played longer, he would have really challenged that record set by Benni McCarthy.

He's one of the gentlemen I've watched over a long time and have been very humbled by. Sometimes in football you get to realise that people forget easily. You know, when he had a rough patch, everybody seemed to have forgotten what a great player he is and was for Kaizer Chiefs. Even when he didn't score a lot of goals between 2019 and when he left, he still scored some crucial goals, and he played a huge role in being a leader on the field of play and working hard for the team. I believe that he needs to be celebrated. He's one of the best we have had in the country, and I wish him all the best going forward.

CHAPTER 15

ADVICE TO YOUNG SOCCER PLAYERS

My first piece of advice to young and upcoming soccer players is to listen attentively, be humble and have a close circle of good people around you all the time.

When a young aspiring player breaks through to the world of professional football, he gets an unimaginable amount of attention from the media, family, friends, and soccer supporters and he also gets financial freedom.

Not everyone is prepared or equipped to deal with the enormity of the limelight you receive when you become a star. After all, you're just a young player starting off your journey in professional football. The sudden attention and financial freedom tend to make some people arrogant, and as a result they end up making grave mistakes. Now, that's the last thing you want if you wish to sustain your career and popularity. It is, therefore, essential that you have a close-knit circle of good people. These could be anyone, from your family and friends and including your mentors and coaches, as well as your advisors and agents.

Remember, when you make it to the top as a professional soccer player, you suddenly get a lot of friends and others with agendas of their own. There is a saying that says, 'Money doesn't change you; it reveals you.'

Some players become arrogant and forget where they come from. You'll come across countless people who will try to trick you to beat you to get to the top. And if you're too rigid and arrogant, you may not be able to handle the complex situations of this highly competitive world. But when you're surrounded by good, sincere people, they'll not only keep you grounded but also give you the best advice for your career and life.

Whether you want to sign a new contract, get a new house, or buy a car, there are a lot of things that a footballer needs to put in place if they are to achieve new heights, both on a personal and professional level. So, if you don't have the right people to give you the right guidance and advice at the right time, you can make mistakes that can cost you badly.

Wrong advice or lack of advice leads to wrong decisions, and they can ruin careers and dreams. So, the most precious advice that I can give to young footballers is to surround yourself with good people who give you valuable advice. They will help you become a better decision-maker, a better player as well as a better person.

SOME ADVICE AROUND THE FOLLOWING

1. Respect
What is respect in football?

Respect yourself, respect your opponents, respect your coach and the officials, and most of all respect the game itself, for all its beauty, inconsistencies, disappointments, and hard-earned joy.

2. Leaving a legacy behind
What does it mean to leave a legacy?

In its simplest terms, your legacy is something meaningful that you give to the people who come after you. You might see the benefits of your actions and gifts while still alive, but the results will continue after your death. Pay it forward.

3. Attitude

Maintaining a positive attitude is very important. You should expect the best in every circumstance, and show a positive attitude towards your teammates, coaches and the management.

4. Soccer Trials

Attending a soccer trial is a very important moment in any aspiring soccer player's life. Be sure to be on time for the trials. When you arrive, introduce yourself to the coach and the technical team. You must arrive already prepared, so pack your equipment, water and a light snack ahead of time. Then, when you arrive, you can concentrate on playing to the best of your ability.

While there, listen, learn, try things out, and explore new things. Use all your senses to absorb everything that you are being taught. Make sure to always go the extra mile. They might be playing you in different positions, but just go for it.

It is important to always stay calm. Trials can be an emotional experience and the pace and new experiences can be overwhelming. Be calm at all times, even when things are not going well.

Remember that you have done everything possible to prepare yourself for this chance, so relax and play your natural game, showcasing your talent and skills in the game. Be confident, but don't overcomplicate things or try to do too much. Concentrate on excelling in your specific role, fulfilling your responsibilities, and supporting your teammates. Coaches are not only interested in your skills but also in your attitude and character.

If the trial does not work out, analyse what could have been done better and then move on to the next opportunity that arises. Don't be afraid to ask the coaches for feedback about why you were not selected. It is your right to know for your own future development.

Remember that soccer is a team sport and that you need to support and encourage your teammates. This makes for better teams and teammates.

5. Joining a professional soccer team

Becoming a professional player takes plenty of blood, sweat and tears, and you need to be 150% committed, right from the very beginning. To become a professional soccer player, you need to dedicate all your time and energy to doing the things that will give you the edge. This includes early morning conditioning, individual skill work, both before and after training, and making sure that you eat, sleep and live properly, taking care of your body and your mind.

You need to accept that the odds are against you and that you are going to have to devote every waking moment of almost every day to making sure that you have the best chance of reaching your dreams.

Here are some things that you can do to help yourself

1. Develop your body physically

You do not need to be built like Lionel Messi, Kylian Mbappé, Neymar da Silva Santos Júnior, or Cristiano Ronaldo to make it in the big leagues. You do need to be well-conditioned and very fit so that you can keep moving around the pitch over long periods. You do need to be athletic, and you have to have stamina. Soccer is about high-intensity movements, and being able to do these can be achieved if you are willing to put in the effort. You need to be able to sprint, change direction, jump and have long-term stamina to keep going over a 90-minute or longer match. Put in the extra mile.

2. Pay attention to what you eat and drink

Feeding your body properly is critical to being fit in both mind and body. You need to ensure that you get proper nutrition from your food and drink. While it is not possible to eat and drink 100% healthily all the time, you do need to pay attention to what you eat, and when you eat it. Stay away from junk food. Go and google and see what junk food is.

3. When injured, take your recovery seriously

Playing and training hard and regularly takes it out of your body. You need to listen carefully to what your body tells you and become familiar with when it is time to rest and recover. If you don't do this, you may get injured and lay to waste everything that you have been training so hard for. In addition to your weekly training schedule, you should consider adding stretching exercises, ice baths, massage and getting extra sleep. Taking time out to relax and let your body recover will allow you to compete at your best during practice sessions and matches.

4. Study the strategies and tactics of soccer

No matter how good a player you are, and how clever your moves and tricks might be, if you don't understand the game or have the tactical discipline to retain your position, you will be a non-starter. If you want to make it to the top, you need to learn everything that you can about soccer strategy and tactics so that you understand what is expected of you. The best way of doing this is to watch videos of your favourite players. Watch how they move on the pitch and how this depends on the ball, what their teammates are doing, and what the opposition is up to. Carefully analysing games will help you to understand when to push up, drop off, take on an opposition player, and so on.

5. Develop and improve your soccer skills daily

No matter how much you might have learned about tactics and strategy, and no matter how fit you have become, you need to keep your skills honed and work on improving them on an ongoing basis. You need to have a soccer ball at your feet all the time. You should be practising things like first touch, ball control, long and short passes, crossing, shooting, heading and tackling as much as possible, working on these until you are confident in your abilities and can stay calm under pressure. And then you also need to work on your decision-making skills so that you know when to use your skills during real matches.

6. Search for opportunities

It is probably not enough to put in great performances at every game. You are probably going to have to be proactive and search for opportunities. It is a good idea to prepare and keep up to date a Curriculum Vitae (CV) that highlights your previous experience as a player. This should include the teams you've played for, your particular achievements, and important statistics about you as a player.

7. Never stop improving

Realising your dreams of signing a professional contract is not the end; it is just a new beginning. You will now have to work even harder to win a spot in the starting 11.

Conclusion

It takes enormous dedication, sacrifice and hard work to become a professional soccer player. Stay dedicated and trust the process but remember that a professional soccer player's life can change in an instant. You could be loaned out to another team or suffer a severe injury. You may even be cut from the team. So, while concentrating on your current career as a professional soccer player, you must make sure that you have something to fall back on if it doesn't work out, like a business or education.

FINANCIAL MANAGEMENT

1. Budgeting is key

Our soccer careers are short. If you spend all your money while you are earning it, you will have nothing when your soccer career comes to an end. You need to plan for your future from the outset, and budget from the very beginning. Put serious thought into what you need to live on a day-to-day basis. Work out what this will cost each month. Make a budget and live within it. Saving what income is left over is very important.

2. Consult with trustworthy financial advisors

As a professional soccer player, chances are that you are not a financial expert and don't have a lot of experience in accounting or investing. Therefore, be sure to get advice from reputable financial advisors. Find advisors and accountants who have experience in the soccer industry and who have a good reputation among your fellow players. Meet a few people before making a decision. Watch out for scammers!

Very few professional soccer players earn enough to be truly worry-free for the rest of their lives. No matter what we earn, we have to live within our means while trying our best to protect our futures by careful planning and investing.

CHAPTER 16

MENTAL PREPARATION
Mental toughness is key in the opening and closing stages of the season.

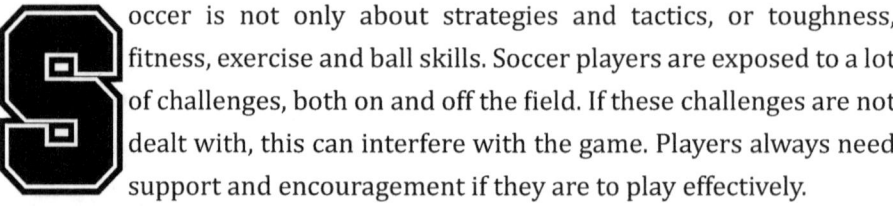

Soccer is not only about strategies and tactics, or toughness, fitness, exercise and ball skills. Soccer players are exposed to a lot of challenges, both on and off the field. If these challenges are not dealt with, this can interfere with the game. Players always need support and encouragement if they are to play effectively.

It is not enough to deal with only the physical side of playing soccer, both the mental and the physical sides should be dealt with. If a player's mental health is good, half of the problems on the field will be solved. It is for this reason that I believe that every team should have a mental coach.

People assume that toughness on the field is all about being fit and physically tough. It is about jumping up every time you get knocked down. But this is not entirely correct. In addition to being physically prepared, toughness includes having a strong mental approach. This includes being able to deal with setbacks, being able to handle losing a game and being able to handle teams and players who behave in an intimidating way. It means being able to stay focused, no matter what else is going on.

Cesc Fabregas said, 'Football is nearly 80% in your mind. You can have the talent but if you don't have the head, you will go nowhere.' I agree with this. If you have the mental toughness to cope with making mistakes (and other people making mistakes), and with things not going your way, you have a far better chance of taking your practice skills to the game and playing at your best.

I have been coached by many coaches. Sometimes I felt alone and rejected. This increased when the goals started to dry up and I felt pressure from the coaches, the management and the supporters. When you feel so alone, anxiety and stress start to take their toll. Some players respond to this by buying fast cars, going to nightclubs partaking in drugs and alcohol or mixing with a bad crowd.

If there is someone to whom you can talk face-to-face, this can make a big difference, so go for it. This must be someone who can help you to focus and to get your composure and confidence back. All the world's top athletes work with life coaches and sports psychologists to develop routines to use before games that include strategies for developing focus, confidence and trust. People like this can help a player to develop a game plan.

Pre-match routines are not one-size-fits-all and should be developed for each sportsperson, taking into account the person and the sport, whether they will be playing at home or away, and the player's preferences.

A pre-match routine may include taking ten minutes to analyse the different situations that may arise before the game starts. You may listen to music that helps you to feel ready and that helps you to transition into the role you must play on the field.

The importance of mental training in sport

You do gym exercises to keep your body in shape. In the same way, some exercises can be done to keep your mental 'muscles' in shape. This can improve what you can achieve with your physical abilities. Mental training works to prepare the mind so that you can perform at your peak. Factors such as focus, confidence, belief in yourself, and the ability to motivate yourself can lift a player to the next level, especially if their physical ability is already there.

Just as you warm up your body before a game, you should make mental preparation a part of your routine. Do mental preparation for issues like how you will handle a wet field, how you will handle a noisy crowd, and how you will handle yourself if you get called to kick a penalty. You must be ready for whatever happens.

The visualisation technique

With the help of Mr Charley Pietersen, my life coach and former chief executive officer of Bloemfontein Celtic FC, I adopted the visualisation technique.

There was a time when I was struggling to score. It was both mentally and physically difficult for me when it seemed that I just couldn't score and that I was not helping my team to win the all-important games. Credit must go to coaches Stuart Baxter and Gavin Hunt, because they kept on believing in me.

With the help of my life coach, I became the leading Kaizer Chiefs scorer in the Premier Soccer League era. I managed to move two goals ahead of club legend Siphiwe Tshabalala on 58 goals. I even scored a brace in a 2–1 win against SuperSport United in a DStv premiership match.

Neither players nor coaches should underestimate how important supporting the mental side of a player is.

When a player steps up to take a free kick and pictures the ball going into the upper corner, he is practising visualisation. Now, while this technique might not pop into your mind when you consider soccer training, it is an excellent way of focusing on achieving a particular goal, especially scoring that crowd-raising spectacular goal that wins the game.

Visualisation is a skill that needs to be practised daily and should become a habit that is used all the time in the life of any professional athlete.

Visualisation in soccer

One of the ways in which I use visualisation is to visualise the game two or three days before it is to be played. Before I do this, I discuss and analyse the opposing team with my teammates and work out strategies for overcoming the strong points and taking advantage of their weaknesses. As a striker, I analyse the keeper and defenders whom I am going to face. Then I take some 'me-time' and visualise myself playing against them, using the strategies, and getting the ball into the net. I see the ball hitting the net – that is what it means to visualise.

When you visualise for yourself, see yourself in the stadium. While you are relaxing, imagine what you want to accomplish in the game the next day. Clearly picture yourself getting ready for the game, putting on your boots, and pulling your jersey on. Picture the crowd. How big is it? Think about what the field will be like, what the weather will be like, and what the crowd will be like. Make your pictures as vivid and detailed as possible. With visualisation, you are in fact training your mind to achieve certain tasks. You must take free kicks and penalties in your mind. You must run and dribble and kick. If you can see it clearly in your mind, you can then do it on the soccer field.

If you get into the habit of always going through what you want to do in your next game before you go to bed, then over time it will get easier and easier and soon you will find yourself automatically visualising moves, plays, and things you want to achieve in the game.

Wayne Rooney said: 'I always like to picture the game the night before. I'll ask the kit man what kit we're wearing, so I can visualise it. It's something I've always done, from when I was a young boy. It helps to train your mind for situations that might happen the following day. I think about it as I'm lying in bed. What will I do if the ball gets crossed in the box this way? What movement will I have to make to get to the end of it? Just different things that might make you 1% sharper.'

What is an affirmation?

People who have a positive mental outlook are more likely to achieve their goals than people who don't. An affirmation is a statement that endorses something.

Positive affirmations are statements that you can use to remove negative thoughts and replace them with positive ones. 'Negative: we always lose against Orlando Pirates. Positive: we always beat Orlando Pirates.' One would rather use positive affirmations than negative affirmations that entrench negative thoughts.

Research has shown that by repeating an affirmation regularly, your mind accepts it as true, and you start to put your words into action. Affirmations are usually phrased as if they are already true, so they are in the present tense. Rather than saying, 'I will become the best player in the team,' an affirmation would be phrased, 'I am the best player in the team'.

It's the repetition of affirmations that leads to belief. And once that belief becomes a deep conviction, things began to happen Muhammad Ali.

Some of my affirmations

1. I love myself.
2. I believe in myself.
3. I am dedicated to and excited about practising.
4. I am an amazing player.
5. I am committed to my training.
6. I always make the starting line-up.
7. I can jump high (header).

8. I am a winner at whatever I compete in.
9. I am faster than the wind.
10. I am a natural goal scorer.
11. I always perform at my best under pressure.
12. I always push myself to be in the starting line-up of every game.
13. My stamina is constantly increasing.
14. I am always focused on winning.
15. I always enjoy the training sessions.
16. I score goals in every game.
17. I naturally focus my mind when I need to concentrate.
18. I am a hard worker.
19. I enjoy practising hard.
20. Motivation is easy for me to find when training.
21. I have a very high level of endurance.
22. I always win and love the feeling of winning.
23. I am a goal-scoring machine.

CHAPTER 17

AFTERWORD BY MRS WENDY PARKER

His journey has been nothing short of incredible. From humble beginnings to becoming one of the most respected players in the PSL.

As his wife and the mother of our two boys, I've had a front-row seat to witness his amazing husband and dad qualities. His passion for soccer, his discipline and his role as a parent have inspired me and our family.

From the moment I met my husband, I could tell how much he loved soccer. His dedication to the sport is admirable and has played a significant role in his success. I've seen how he puts in long hours of training and preparation for every game. His enthusiasm for soccer is contagious, as he is always eager to share his love and knowledge of the sport with our family and up and coming players. He has also demonstrated a remarkable level of perseverance through his injuries and setbacks, which has taught me and the boys to never give up on our own goals.

His level of professionalism and commitment in his soccer career is what sets him apart. He never takes shortcuts and always gives his best effort, whether on or off the field. His discipline extends beyond his soccer career; it has also made him a responsible, reliable and dedicated husband and father figure, not only to our two boys but other young men.

He sets a great example for our children by instilling in them the values of discipline, commitment and dedication. He puts God first in all that he does.

My husband's loving, kind and supportive qualities are what I cherish most. He spends quality time with our boys, even in the midst of his busy schedule, and prioritises his family above everything else.

He admires and respects me as his wife and goes out of his way to make me feel special. His love for his family is unwavering, and he always puts our needs first. Bernard is admired, loved and forever cherished. Thank you, Bernard, for sharing your story! Keep on persevering. 👏

CHAPTER 18

ACCOLADES & AWARDS

Kaizer Chiefs 2011-2022

Debut Vs Bidvest Wits, 7th August 2011 MTN 8 Quarterfinal, Kaizer Chiefs 2 Bidvest Wits 1

Final game for Kaizer Chiefs, 21st May 2022, DStv Premiership, Kaizer Chiefs 2 Swallows FC 2

The first goal for Kaizer Chiefs, scored on debut converted a penalty in an MTN 8 Quarterfinal against Bidvest Wits on the 7th of August 2011.

Final goal for Kaizer Chiefs, 21st May 2022, DStv Premiership, Scored the second goal for Chiefs levelling the game at 2-2

Appearances for Kaizer Chiefs in all competitions: 359
Goals for Kaizer Chiefs in all competitions: 62

Kaizer Chiefs all-time top scorer in the PSL Era from 1996-97 in all competitions.

Became Chiefs all-time top scorer in the PSL Era when he scored a brace in a 2-1 win over SuperSport United in a league game on the 24th October 2021 away from home.

Scored 12 goals in 28 league games in the 2012-13 season as Chiefs won their first league title in 7 years.

Scored four goals in Chiefs opening league game of the 2012-13 season as Chiefs defeated AmaZulu 6-0, Chiefs biggest win of the PSL Era in a league game.

Honours with Kaizer Chiefs (4): 2012-13 League Winner, 2012-13 Nedbank Cup Winner / South African Cup, 2014-15 MTN 8 Winner, 2014-15 League Winner, 2020-21 CAF Champions League Runner Up.

Played in 30 Soweto derbies-Kaizer Chiefs vs Orlando Pirates

Information provided by Kaizer Chiefs (Mr Yusuf Muhammad)

2009/10 Eredivisie Champion,

2010 Johan Cruyff Shield winner (both with FC Twente)

2012/13 league winner, 2014/15 league winner, 2012/13 Nedbank Cup winner, 2014 MTN8 winner.

In the 2013/14 season, he won the Lesley Manyathela Golden Boot award with 10 goals.

2020/21 CAF Champions League runner-up

2013, 2016, 2017, and 2021 Carling Black Label Cup winner (all with Chiefs)

2013/14 PSL Golden Boot winner (10 goals)

2014 CHAN Golden Boot winner, played in 2009 FIFA Confederations Cup, played in 2010 FIFA World Cup, played in 2013 Afcon.

ARTICLE ON CRISTIANO RONALDO

10 Exciting Life Lessons You Must Learn From Cristiano Ronaldo (winnersstory.com)

https://winnersstory.com/life-lessons-cristiano-ronaldo/

Cristiano Ronaldo is one of the greatest footballers of all time. He has been an inspiration for many people around the world.

Born from a poor family, he entered the stage of football and has been ruling it for almost two decades. With five Ballon d 'Or awards and many more to come, he showed the world why he is the best.

Ronaldo showed continuous progress throughout his career, right from starting his professional football career with Sporting CP to re-joining Manchester United.

There are many things we can learn from him, and we have gathered 10 important life lessons we can learn from Cristiano Ronaldo.

1. Spend quality time with your family

Ronaldo is a family man. He spends quality time with his family even with his hectic schedule and he loves to play with his children. He often credits his success to his mother. She has been the backbone throughout his career.

Having a supportive family is a great thing for a person. They are the ones who care the most for us. So, it's very important to spend quality time with your family. Enjoy your time with them, which helps you to relieve the stress and helps you to achieve more in your life.

2. Have a goal in your life

Ronaldo, from childhood, had a clear goal of what he wanted to do in life, to be a professional footballer. And as he became a professional footballer, his next target was to become the best footballer in the world.

Patrice Evra in an interview talked about the conversation with Ronaldo, "When he won his first Ballon d'Or, he said, I have to win at least five."

The important lesson that we have to learn here is "having goals in life". Most of us don't know what we want to do in life. We just go with the flow and end up procrastinating many things in our lives.

Instead, we should set our goals first and break them down into small milestones and reach them one by one. When we reach our goal, improve on that and aim for the next one.

Remember, without destiny in your mind, you don't have control over your travel.

3. Do hard work with focus and dedication

Ronaldo today did not arrive overnight. There is a lot of hard work behind it. His dedication and focus on the game started way back from his childhood and continues till now. He practices day and night to improve his skillset and be the best version of himself.

Even during game days, he goes for training after the game. He will be the first one to enter and the last person to leave in every training session.

He does not give excuses and he practises every single day.

Former Portugal coach, Carlos Queiroz on Ronaldo, "There are some great players that have so much belief that when things are not going well on the training field they just stop. They think, 'I am good, today is not right, but tomorrow it will be fine! They never think there could be a problem. Not

Cristiano. He works and works until everything goes right and only then he's satisfied."

So, success cannot come overnight or just by only dreaming. We need to put our dream into action consistently. With continuous hard work, we can achieve anything in life, and it applies to every career path we choose.

4. Believe in yourself and build super confidence

"I never tried to hide the fact that my only goal is to be the best."

Ronaldo shows a lot of confidence both on and off the field. From childhood, he had a strong self-belief that he would be a professional footballer. And he wants to be the best.

He always had faith in himself and without it, he would not have reached greater heights.

He tells openly what he wants to be and puts all his hard work into that and never compromises.

We always want to achieve something in life. But the biggest drawback in doing so is self-doubt. Most of us doubt ourselves and don't have the confidence to work on our goals. We work for some days and when the results are not coming, we lose our confidence and move away.

Having talent is a great thing but if you don't show it to the world, it's no use. Be super confident in your ability and show the world.

5. Learn continuously and adapt to the changes

When Ronaldo played for Sporting CP, he impressed Manchester United players with his dribbling skills during their friendly match. This paved the way for Manchester United to sign him.

He was known for dribbling in the initial phase of his career such as the stepovers and the famous Ronaldo 'chops!'

As he moved, he underwent a major physical transformation, developing a muscular body, to improve his strength and jumping ability that made him an aerial threat in the penalty area. He also became a set-piece specialist and an effective goal-scorer.

And he kept changing his game as he became older, like dribbling less but his energy remained high.

The important life lesson from Cristiano Ronaldo here is, to never stop learning. You can be an expert on a particular topic, but you cannot survive with that in the long run. Change yourself, adapt to the changes, play with your strengths, and keep on learning. Nobody can stop you.

6. Have a positive attitude in life and don't mind the criticism from the haters

Ronaldo has always been described as having an arrogant image on the pitch by the media. And his haters used to describe him, that he is not a naturally skilled footballer.

With all these negative sounds around him, nothing bothered Ronaldo. He looked at them with a positive mindset and kept on improving his game. Now many of his earlier haters are fans of him.

"I don't mind people hating me, because it pushes me."

Criticism and haters are part of our life. We might have changed or might have left doing what we loved to do because of negative comments around us. But we should never let any criticism go to our heads.

Just focus on what we want to achieve in our life and never stop.

7. Leave your comfort zone and enter the growth zone

At a young age, Ronaldo moved from his hometown to Lisbon to join a youth football academy. He was homesick during those days, but he continued to focus on the game.

At the age of 14, he agreed with his mother to discontinue his education to focus only on football. He believed that he had the ability to play professional football.

Comfort is the main roadblock to anyone's success. We cannot achieve anything by simply staying in our comfort zone. We need to sacrifice something to achieve something.

If we want to be fit, get out of bed by 5 am and hit the gym. To be healthy, remove those junk foods. To be a musician, sacrifice those TV times and practice with your instruments.

Anything is possible in life if we sacrifice.

8. Take care of your health and be fit

One of the important life lessons we all can learn from Cristiano Ronaldo is fitness.

Ronaldo is one of the fittest athletes in the world and has been an inspiration for millions. He maintains a strict diet and does not consume alcohol.

He improved his fitness throughout his career which helped him to keep his game on high and relatively injury-free.

When Ronaldo joined Juventus, his medical report has been compared to that of a 20-year-old. His body fat was just 7% when compared to other footballers, where their average is around 10 or 11%. His muscle mass was 50% which is around 4% higher than other footballers of his age.

To add to that, he recorded a top sprint speed of 33.9 kph during the 2018 FIFA World Cup, which was faster than anyone in the tournament.

As we know the famous saying, "Health is wealth". If we take care of our health, it will take care of other things in our lives.

Having healthy foods and exercising regularly gives us the physical and mental energy to be at our best throughout our lives.

9. Be a leader and focus on your team's success

Ronaldo has many leadership qualities like taking the pressure during critical situations like penalties, supporting his teammates, setting benchmarks in training, and hunger to be the best. And above all gaining the trust of the teammates.

For him the team comes first, his target is always to win the game. Even though he has scored many goals in his career, he equally assisted many goals for the team.

Leadership is an important quality one should possess. You don't need to be the best talent to lead the team. As long as you have respect from the team and the attitude you show, you can be a great leader.

Always think about your team goals first then your individual targets.

10. Get a mentor and learn from them

When Ronaldo joined Manchester United, he was just 18 years old. He had the talent but to guide him on the right path he needed a mentor.

Sir Alex Ferguson was the one who played a key element in the development of Ronaldo.

"He's been my father in sport, one of the most important and influential factors in my career!"

Similar to Ronaldo, we need a mentor in our life. They will help us to see both sides of the coin or show us the different views altogether.

We need to be open to feedback to achieve success.

ARTICLES ON PARKER

STATEMENT FROM KAIZER CHIEFS ON SOCIAL MEDIA PLATFORMS

3 June 2022 at 3:23 PM ·

Player Updates:

Kaizer Chiefs will sadly not renew Bernard Parker's contract when it expires at the end of June 2022. Parker, a bona fide Kaizer Chiefs legend, will leave the club he has served with distinction for 11 years.

He joined Chiefs in 2011 from the Eredivisie side, FC Twente, and his glittering career saw him play 359 matches for Amakhosi and found the net 62 times.

His exceptional talent and leadership helped Amakhosi to win four major trophies, including two league titles. His professionalism, both on and off the field, is an objective example to any aspiring young footballer.

Thank you for your great service and dedication to the Club, 'Hond'. You remain a true legend.

#ThankYouParker #Amakhosi4Life

SOCIAL MEDIA RESPONSES KAIZER CHIEFS SUPPORTERS AFTER THE ANNOUNCEMENT THAT PARKER IS NO LONGER A CHIEFS PLAYER

Asemahle Lee Van Zly

This guy was a hard-working person and disciplined, I understand why the team kept him for so long, so much respect for you booi.

Mnumzane Zikode Nkwanyana

Parker deserves to be part of Chiefs even if it's not as a Football player. He Gave this club all his heart - you could see it on his face when he was on the field .....

I remember there was a time when some fans used to tease him and say "He celebrates other people's goals like they've won a cup." That's how passionate he was about his job at the club. **BucksFan**

Themba Zizi Jama

Thank you so much Mr. Parker for winning those major trophies for us as Kaizer Chiefs supporters. I will never forget that important winning goal you scored against Supersport United in the Nedbank Cup final. We wish you all the best.

Tshwanelo Mabelane

This is sad. Parker is still one of the most valuable players Kaizer Chiefs has and can still contribute more in the coming seasons.

Mabotsa Shashape

He Played A Huge Part...In Kaizer Chiefs. We Gonna Miss You "The Hond" Much Appreciated By Some Of Us.

Tar Chusta INdlamlenze

They will regret, this is the only player who fought for the badge even though fans didn't like him for whatever reason. Baxter was right.

Mbengeni Jonas Nemakhavhani

Why can't he be given a Job in the development of Kaizer Chiefs this guy is so disciplined and a hardworking guy?

Dimomza Kekana

Bernard Parker is the greatest player that I have seen since supporting Kaizer Chiefs. He always put an effort in on the pitch and he was one of the players that could have died for Chiefs on the pitch. We always say good things come and go, so you were the good thing that we had in Naturena and now you are leaving. But otherwise, good luck with your next chapter and we will always love "De Hond." #loveandpeace

Buda P Mfusi

Very sad. He deserved one last season with Chiefs. Nonetheless, well-done bro for representing the badge well. Well wishes on your future endeavours.

Charley Pietersen

Parker Returns to Play His 30th Soweto Derby-5 MARCH, 2022

Kaizer Chiefs attacker Bernard Parker enters the history books as he will be playing in his 30th official Soweto Derby match since he joined Amakhosi ahead of the 2011-12 season after his return from the Netherlands where he played for FC Twente.

The attacking player missed Amakhosi's last game against Baroka due to a minor injury.

Today's Soweto Derby between Kaizer Chiefs and Orlando Pirates is the 175th official meeting since 1970. Chiefs won the last two league games in 2021. The game in March 2021 ended 1-0 with Samir Nurković scoring the goal and in November Keagan Dolly scored a brace in his first derby. The final score was 2-1. Both matches were played at FNB Stadium.

Parker on the cusp of Soweto Derby milestone

Mar 3, 2022 - 06:58 am KickOff By Staff Reporter

Kaizer Chiefs stalwart Bernard Parker is on the cusp of achieving a remarkable milestone against Soweto derby rivals Orlando Pirates.

Arch-rivals Kaizer Chiefs and Orlando Pirates are set to meet for the 175th time on Saturday when the two giants of South African football go head-to-head in the latest instalment of the highly anticipated Soweto derby.

Veteran Amakhosi forward Bernard Parker featured in 29 of those encounters and could make his 30th appearance for Chiefs against the Buccaneers this weekend after recovering from an injury that ruled him out of the win over Baroka last time out.

Ahead of the encounter, the 35-year-old highlighted his pride at reaching the 30-game mark against the old enemy and revealed that the derby was the type of match that he lived to play in as a professional footballer.

"I am very proud to reach such a milestone," Parker told the club's official **website** on Wednesday. "It is always with joy and a host of other good emotions that I look ahead to this game. The build-up, the hype, the talk, the history… it's an exciting feeling.

"I am happy to be back and always ready to play in these types of games. We live for these games – you want to be involved in this game because it is one of the biggest derbies on the continent. It is always an honour to play in this match."

The former Bafana Bafana star also admitted that he hated losing against Pirates and that one of his favourite outings in the derby came last season when he had the honour of captaining Chiefs in the 100th league edition of the world-famous fixture.

"One of the best derbies I featured in was captaining the team in the 100th league derby last season, which we won," he added. "While I would describe these games as always being a nerve-wracking encounter, I never want to lose against Pirates."

Kaizer Chiefs news: Parker has an appetite for the Soweto Derby

Kaizer Chiefs utility player Bernard Parker is thrilled to be returning to the lineup in time for the Soweto derby on the weekend.-by James-02-03-2022

Bernard Parker of Kaizer Chiefs during the DStv Premiership 2021/22 match between Kaizer Chiefs and Baroka FC on 25 August 2021 at the FNB Stadium, Johannesburg Photo: Muzi Ntombela

Kaizer Chiefs utility player Bernard Parker is thrilled to be returning to the lineup in time for the Soweto derby.

Parker has been influential in past Soweto derbies and hopes to do so again this weekend.

KAIZER CHIEFS VETERAN READY FOR ANOTHER SOWETO DERBY

The versatile Kaizer Chiefs stalwart cannot contain his excitement at the possibility of facing the team's arch-rivals again in what would be his 30th Soweto Derby.

"Yes, I am happy to be back and always ready to play in these types of games. We live for these games – you want to be involved in this game because it is one of the biggest Derbies on the continent. It is always an honour to play in this match," Parker said in an interview with the club website.

MARKING A MILESTONE

Parker is also gearing up for what will be his 21st league game against Orlando Pirates.

"I am very proud to reach such a milestone. It is always with joy and a host of other good emotions that I look ahead to this game. The build-up, the hype, the talk, the history... it's an exciting feeling," says Parker.

Parker said that Kaizer Chiefs never want to suffer the pain of losing when facing the Sea Robbers.

"One of the best derbies I featured in was captaining the team in the 100th league derby last season, which we won. While I would describe these games as always being a nerve-wracking encounter, I never want to lose against Pirates," said Parker.

KAIZER CHIEFS KNOW HOW TO BEAT ORLANDO PIRATES

Parker is also well-accustomed on how to manage play against Pirates.

"With Pirates' style of play and movement, they can always be a hiccup. They have good flair. How to contain that is a challenge. With my experience I know how to contain and manage that," adds Parker.

Kaizer Chiefs and Orlando Pirates are locked in a struggle for the second CAF Champions League place adding to the Soweto Derby.

"It's very, very crucial for us to win. I had a conversation with Daniel Cardoso, we believe winning will set the tone and be a massive confidence booster for us to gain momentum. Winning will lift everything in us for us to get into the CAF Champions League," he emphasised.

WHY PARKER DESERVES MORE RESPECT

KICKOFF JANUARY 2022 NUMBER 537 By Hosea Ramphekwa

On October 24, 2021, Bernard Parker wrote his name into Kaizer Chiefs' history books. Not only did his brace against SuperSport United garner Chiefs a 2-1 victory, but it also engraved his name into the AmaKhosi folklore as he became the club's all-time record goalscorer in the PSL era with 60 goals.

Parker also holds the record for most appearances by a Chiefs player since the PSL's inception as he closes in on 350. Is it a cliche that Kaizer Chiefs forward Bernard Parker is maturing like a fine wine?

At 35, the former Bafana Bafana star is leading from the front with second-to-none commitment and determination. Since joining Chiefs over a decade ago, Parker has seen it all. When AmaKhosi soared to greater heights with trophies flowing to when they dipped in form with a trophy drought, Parker was there as a regular feature. Parker has been a mainstay in black and gold and his longevity in the game is impressive. Years after some of his peers have hung their boots, the man from Reiger Park in Boksburg continues to lace his boots and dish out solid performances. So, what sets Parker apart? "My mindset," Parker says in a past interview. "Your mindset is everything if you want to stay long in the game. I have played with players that were more talented than me; players who were faster than me, stronger than me, and that I shared a position.

"The players that took me off my position throughout the years. I last long because of my mindset, looking after yourself in terms of your body, which is your main tool. You must be the CEO of yourself, which I protect in that way, looking after my body, making sure I eat properly.

"I recover well and am also mindful of what I consume. It can be water to alcohol but there should be a balance. There should be a balance throughout and make sure you are in the best condition ever whenever you step on the field of play."

"HE MIGHT NOT BE IN THE GAME BUT FOR ME HIS WORK RATE IS ONE OF THE THINGS THAT HE ALWAYS GIVES YOU."

'We Played the Cup Together'

Parker became a household name playing his street in the country's finest venues and top arenas abroad. One of the players who knew Parker before his fame, Tsepo Masilela, saw his former teammate at Benoni Premier United go all the way. "When we started playing together, it was in the National First Division for Benoni. We also started playing for the national under-23s at the same time. We saw that things are going in the right direction but back then you could only dream. You never know how things will end up, so you just believe and give it your all.

"Luckily the dream came true, if I can put it that way. We if not yet perfect careers, but we played overseas, We played in the World Cup together in the Confederations Cup. It's a nice story to tell when you sit back and look at where we come from," reflects Masilela.

The AmaZulu defender, who aside from Benoni was also Parker's teammate at Chiefs and Bafana Bafana has seen the striker at work. "He's a hard worker and disciplined guy. As in elite, it's an important aspect of your career, the discipline on and off the field. If you have that, with working hard, it's great because talent alone won't get you anywhere.

Most of the players who shared the dressing room with Parker remark about his work ethic, something that complements his talent immensely. "Every game he gives you what he has on the day. He might not be in the game but for me, his work rate is one of the things that he always gives you. Each and every game that he plays and even in training sessions, he likes working hard," says Reneilwe Letsholonyane, Parker's former teammate at Chiefs.

"His lifestyle of the field is proper, the dedication, the respect, and the love that he has for the game. It goes back to the work that he puts in even when given an opportunity to do what he loves, whether it's at training, playing friendly games, or official games. He would give you a 110% work rate."

Social Media Criticism

Throughout his stay at Chiefs Parker has played a pivotal role for the club. He was an instrumental figure when Chiefs won the ABSA Premiership Title during the 2012/13 and 2014/15 seasons. His goals and assists proved vital as Chiefs won Nedbank Cup and the MTN8 as well.

But when Chiefs blew hot and cold with performances that saw the trophies going everywhere but Naturena, the 35-year-old became one of the most maligned players.

One of his biggest errors, a poor decision against ultimate champions Mamelodi Sundowns during the 2019/20 season, saw him become a victim of slavery on social media, with many blaming him for squandering a chance that could have turned the fortunes of Chiefs in the quest to win the league title.

So intense has been Parker's criticism on social media did Chiefs skipper revealed he had to delete his social media apps and block some of his friends, who were sharing negative memes about him.

"People can learn from the positive attitude that he always has. There are times when the team did not play well and when you check on social media, one of the people getting the stick from supporters would be Parker, solely because he has been there at Chiefs for a long time.

He kept being positive. He still works hard. He still does the things that he needs to do says Letsholonyane. "He's got a big heart. Mentally, he is strong. To be honest, if you have played for this long, sometimes football is a game of pressure. It teaches you more about life and it makes you strong as a person. He's got a big heart and a strong mentality. He keeps on going," observes Masilela.

'Parker is a leader'

Former Chiefs Midfielder Willard Katsande was not spared the punches dished out by disgruntled supporters. The Zimbabwean international says he and Parker laughed off the berating and set their sights on lifting the team. "We told each other that we just need to keep on working hard. We know that the situation with us, it's always against us meaning there is something good about us.

Let's just pull each other, Let's just talk. Let's try to find a common solution for us to overcome this kind of situation." says Katsande.

"Parker is always focused. He always spreads positivity. Psychologically, he's a leader and reads the situation. He knows how to inject energy into the group. Even during moments in the game, you would see us standing together and I would ask him what to do I think we need to do, and he would sometimes ask me the same.

"Then we quickly fixed the thing. Mentally, he is one of the top strong guys with the capacity to deal with all these things that come his way."

Katsande, who left Chiefs to join Sekhukhune United after a decade at Naturena, reveals that he used to spend hours with Parker over coffee as they plotted the fall of the opponents.

During Chief's impressive run in the CAF Champions League, Parker and Katsande chilled and chatted tactics in Casablanca, where they face Moroccan giants Wydad Casablanca.

"Even after dinner, a day before the match when everybody was gone, we sat for 30 to 45 minutes talking about 'what do you think we will need to do with these guys that we are facing.'

"We discussed it and with the level of our understanding, you can see that we've been long in the game. We were not just footballers, we were brothers. We are now family. We were there for each other every time. Even to this day, we still keep in touch. When he scored his two goals (against Supersport), I even sent him a message to say, 'Brother, you really deserve this,' I wish to give him my 16 goals for Chiefs so that he can add to his tally even more," says the midfield hardman.

Parker is one of the few players that are blessed with the ability to use both left and right foot with equal effectiveness. This has enabled him to play various positions. The 2013/14 Lesley Manyathela Golden Boot winner can play as a left winger, right winger, a central midfielder a second striker, a playmaker, and a center forward.

His versatility and willingness to work for the team have seen him survive at Chiefs, where he played under a number of coaches.

"Every day Parker shows up. Sometimes your best ability is availability. He is always available to help the team and that shows what kind of a person he is. He is a good human being," says Masilela. "If you check, sometimes he plays as a winger. He's not the guy who complains. He can play as a striker, number 10, or a right-winger. He is one of the players you dream to have on your team. He is not selfish.

"There's also something that many people don't know about him is that, if you have watched over the years, he has been trying to help the team by playing different positions. Whenever the coach asks him to play a certain position, he gives his best. The effort is always there." Katsande adds; "You can see even when he runs, he runs like a 16-year-old. He never complains and wherever you play him, he always plays. Even if you say go play as a goalkeeper, the guy will always be dedicated. He gives his all so it's not easy to find these kinds of players in this era."

HOW PARKER HELPED BILLIAT REGAIN HIS FORM

Kaizer Chiefs playmaker, Khama Billiat appears to be rediscovering the form that once had made him one of the most feared attackers in the PSL.

Since joining Chiefs, Billiat has not lived up to expectations after his sterling performance at Mamelodi Sundowns, where he was a key figure in their trophy haul. However so far this season there are glimpses of Billiat's brilliance. His impressive form has coincided with his fellow attackers Bernard Parker and Keagan Dolly.

With the trio in attack, Amakhosi have been marauding and menacing. Former Chiefs and Sundowns midfielder Jabulani Mendu is of the view that Parker's influence and Dolly's arrival have been a breath of fresh air for the Zimbabwean international.

"Parker has been consistent, and he has been there when everything was going bad Mendu tells Kick Off. "He has always been there when he's needed, and he has been brilliant since signing for Amakhosi.

"Any team would be lucky to sign Khama. Technically he is brilliant, it's just that he was not motivated in his first two seasons at Chiefs. Now Khama has been doing well and Parker has been doing well too.

"Now do you have that understanding because they played together. They understand one another and Parker is smart. He is experienced and I am sure he has had talks with Khama and other players in the team.

"When Parker is on the field of play everybody has confidence. He is a leader and he just doesn't lead on the field of play because he's wearing an armband. You can feel that he is a father figure, especially to those youngsters that are coming from the development ranks. It's going to be a loss to Chiefs to lose a player of Parker's calibre when he finally leaves."

"IF YOU RESPECT THE GAME, THE GAME RESPECTS YOU."

No Recognition

Parker's football resume is laden with impressive feats. He campaigned for South Africa at the 2009 FIFA Confederations Cup 2010 Soccer World Cup, 2013 Africa Cup of Nations, and 2014 Africa Cup of Nations, where he was the top scorer in the 2015 Africa Cup of Nations.

Parker is tied in third with Katlego Mphela on the country's all-time leading scorer charts with 23 goals from 73 appearances. Naturally, players over the age of 30 tend to slow down owing to a loss of pace in potency, but that doesn't seem to be the case with Parker.

"The guy is always hungry. When you are hungry you don't think about what you did yesterday, and you only think about how you need to better your game. We used to do extra sessions, before and after sessions, to keep our bodies sharp and to cope with the younger ones.

"It shows you how much we respect the game. If you respect the game, the game respects you. That's why he is still performing at a higher level at a big team," says Katsande.

Katsande, Letsholonyane, and Masilela sing from the same hymnbook in declaring that Parker, who was the league champion in Netherlands' Eredivisie with FC Twente in the 2009/10 season, still has a lot to offer Chiefs and the country at large.

"If he was my player, I would definitely play him because of the role that he plays as a leader in the team, the work that he puts in every game and the positive attitude that he has, even when things are not going well.

"For me, he has a lot to give to football in the country and to help the young ones to see that when somebody works hard, they are rewarded. People see it in Parker. They don't hear that, 'I work hard,' They see it. That's what he does every day," states Letsholonyane, whose sentiments are echoed by Masilela.

"He is someone who tries to always perform whenever he is given a chance. He's a senior player and he has up-and-coming players that look up to him. He's just got to be a good role model and continue to be a good person. We all know what he has done throughout his career," Masilela says.

Parker's hard work has gone beyond the playing field. Despite his hectic schedule as a player, husband, and father, he has been furthering his education.

In 2019 Parker obtained a qualification in Sports Management from Boston City Campus and Business College. In 2021, the striker got a Higher Certificate in Sports Marketing, and he is currently studying towards a qualification in Sports Psychology.

"Parker is the type of a guy that all youngsters in South Africa, not only Chiefs, need to look up to him and find out how did this guy work on this path. From there, they will draw inspiration," says Katsande, who feels Parker is not given the respect due to him.

"He is a top professional and I don't think he gets the recognition he deserves. I think he deserves better, but you know how it is when you are someone, sometimes your coverage is limited because of who you are.

"For me, those are the people who deserve recognition because they've been on top of their game for more than 10 seasons. The guy had played in Europe, in the Champions League, and he came here to rub his experience off on the young ones.

Parker equals Mooki and Khune 24 AUGUST 2021

Bernard Parker began his 11th league campaign with Kaizer Chiefs by captaining Amakhosi as they drew 0-0 with TS Galaxy in their opening league game on Sunday, in the process making history and setting another important milestone with the club.

Parker joined a select group of Chiefs players who have managed to feature in 10 opening league games of a new season with Chiefs in the PSL era, joining Thabo Mooki and Itumeleng Khune as players since 1996-97 who have featured the most times in the opening league game of a different season for Chiefs.

Since joining Chiefs ahead of the 2011-12 season, Parker only missed out on starting the opening game in the 2014-15 season and has featured in the team's opening league game in 10 of 11 seasons, with Sunday's game being the seventh season in succession that he featured in Chiefs opening league game.

Only Mooki and Willard Katsande, who featured in the opening league games in nine successive campaigns, and Khune, who played in 8 opening league games in succession, have featured in more successive league games for Chiefs in their opening league games of a PSL season.

For Parker – who was this week named as club vice-captain for the season by coach Stuart Baxter – the match against TS Galaxy was his 260th league appearance for Chiefs and his 355th game for the club overall. He has scored 58 goals in these games and one more goal will see him overtake Siphiwe Tshabalala as Chief's all-time top scorer in the PSL era in all competitions.

He will also be looking to catch up to Tshabalala and become the Club's leading scorer in league games since the formation of the PSL. Currently, Parker has scored 45 league goals for Chiefs while Tshabalala has 49.

Parker recently said in an interview with www.kaizerchiefs.com that "wherever the coach will put me, every time you see Bernard Parker, he will give his 120% for the team."

They Said That About Shabba & Yeye – Baxter

Oct 25, 2021 – Soccer Laduma-By Mazola Molefe

Bernard Parker's two goals for Kaizer Chiefs in the victory over SuperSport United at the weekend have earned him even more respect from coach Stuart Baxter.

The one-time Bafana Bafana frontman rolled back the years on Sunday as he twice beat goalkeeper Ronwen Williams to hand the Glamour Boys a 2-1 win, which moved them up to fifth place on the DStv Premiership table.

Some Chiefs fans who celebrated weren't always Parker praise singers, particularly over the course of the previous season when they struggled under then-coach Gavin Hunt as the player entered the final year of his contract.

"There are two issues there, without wanting to sound like I am having a swipe at anybody. I just think that we are living and playing football in a time where it's quick fixes and instant success," Baxter told journalists.

"When you've worked as hard as Bernard has, it's very easy for people to say you are over the top or not up to it. They've been saying that for quite a long time – they said that about 'Shabba' (Siphiwe Tshabalala), seven years before he retired. They said it about 'Yeye' (Reneilwe Letsholonyane) and (many) of other players, and these are the two (who) came back and proved people wrong."

The Englishman knows Parker better than most, having worked with him in his first spell at Chiefs between 2012 and 2015, winning the league with the veteran at his peak, then following his return from FC Twente in Holland.

Baxter has said Parker will be captain whenever goalkeeper Itumeleng Khune is not selected in the starting line-up.

"That's the one thing, and we have to live with that as players and coaches because that is society and the world we live in at the moment. I've just said to the players that they are privileged to have a senior professional like Bernard Parker, who puts in the shift that he put in tonight and gets the two goals that win us the three points," the coach said, seemingly having a go at the social media trolls who've made it a habit to complain about Parker.

"He is an absolute glowing example of the sort of players we want to produce in SA – hardworking, humble, good team player, responsible in society, and for that reason alone Bernard Parker is worth a place at Kaizer Chiefs. But he is more than that. He is still a very competitive player. Will he play every game when everybody is fit? I don't know. But certainly, Bernard is one of those players who are a pleasure to have around the club."

Emotional Bernard Parker on Breaking Kaizer Chiefs Record - iDiski Times

Bernard Parker was visibly emotional after breaking Siphiwe Tshabalala's all-time record for Kaizer Chiefs after years of "negativity".

The 35-year-old scored both goals in Amakhosi's 2-1 win at SuperSport United on Sunday, taking his Chiefs tally to **60** in the PSL era.

The brace was Parker's first two goals in the DStv Premiership and as a consequence, he's overtaken Shabba's 58 goals.

"I just want to thank God that I managed to break the record," he told *SuperSport TV* after the match.

"Thanks to everyone, especially my family, who've always been there for me through tough times.

"Big up to the lads that we managed to stay strong, we managed to close the spaces, knowing that SuperSport is a dangerous team and how well they've done so far.

"This is a massive win and I believe there is more to come from us."

Parker, though, had to go off injured and explained he left everything on the pitch.

"What the coach has asked from me to make runs behind them," he added.

"As I mentioned earlier on in our movement, which was very key, which was very important. I tried to do as much movement as possible for the team and I got the goals.

"I tried to do more and unfortunately, I got injured. It's now back to recovery and shift our focus back onto the next game."

The Chiefs veteran got emotional when asked what it meant to break Tshabalala's record, referring to the criticism he's received over the years.

"Thank you very much, I just want to send a shoutout to my people who have been there for me through all the negativity I got over the last years," he explained.

"Thank you for always believing in me especially my wife and thanks to God."

McGregor congratulates Bernard Parker on Kaizer Chiefs record (kickoff.com)

Pitso Mosimane ✓
@TheRealPitso

They call him, "Die Hond". You have consistently given everything in this game for many years. Class is permanent. Salute! @BernardParker .

7:02 pm · 25 Oct 2021 · Twitter for iPad

McGregor congratulates Parker on Chiefs record.

Oct 26, 2021 - 08:00 pm By Sipho Mlotha

Kaizer Chiefs legend Shane McGregor has congratulated the club's captain Bernard Parker for his latest achievement.

Besides walking away with the man of the match in yesterday's 2-1 over SuperSport United, 'Die Hond's' brace saw him overtaking Siphiwe Tshabalala as Amakhosi's all-time leading goal scorer in the Premier Soccer League era after scoring his 60th goal. Tshabalala who has since retired sits at 58.

"Well done to him, I mean to do something like that is very difficult, and obviously congratulations to him," McGregor tells **Kickoff.com.** "It hasn't been easy, but as you know he's been playing well of late, so yes congratulations on that, it's a big achievement.

"I think now it's the hard work he's been putting in and the experience you know. He's learned what the game is about, and he knows exactly what he needs to do.

"Yes, the team went through a bad patch, but I think it's the hard work that made the big change at the moment.

"He seems to be gelling well with the rest of the players they are forming a good combination at the moment, so I think he had a lot to do with it. You know at times when you haven't got the right players around you it makes your job a bit harder. I think because of Dolly, because of Billiat it has made it easier for him. I've been quite impressed with his work rate." Macgregor says he does not see any reason why the 35-year-old cannot carry on at least for another season.

"I can't answer for him you know; I don't know how he feels but the way he's working and the way he's looking you know I don't see why not. Unfortunately, we all know how football is, at a certain age it's getting harder every week.

"But yes, he's done well in the past couple of weeks, it looks to be hard work, to be honest with you." Parker has now scored three goals so far this season in all competitions.

Thanda Royal Zulu claim revenge

Thanda Royal Zulu claim revenge (iol.co.za) By Feb 14, 2008

Germiston - After an extended break, due to the recently concluded Africa Cup of Nations, Thanda Royal Zulu ended their jinx when they beat Kaizer Chiefs 1-0 in an ABSA Premiership game played at Olympia Park Stadium in Rustenburg on Wednesday night. It was a sweet revenge for the KwaZulu Natal outfit which lost 2-0 to AmaKhosi in their first round.

Both teams went into this game with the clear intention of starting the second round on a high note.

Chiefs were impressive in their forward forays with Tinashe Nengomasha, and Thabo Mooki orchestrating operations as they swamped the Natal visitors' territory in search of an early goal. Thanda Zulu Royal also looked dangerous on the few raids they launched and had Chiefs rearguard reeling as they piled on the pressure.

Former Kaizer Chiefs Ivorian striker, Serge Djiehoua, was a constant thorn for the AmaKhosi defence and Chiefs Thuso Phala caused considerable concern for Thanda Royal's roadblock.

The first real chance of the game fell in the path of Phala in the 11th minute, after a good interchange with Simphiwe Tshabalala, but his shot went wide.

Thanda Royal Zulu retaliated with some good moves, and in the 21st minute, Bernard Parker watched in disbelief when his well-taken shot was acrobatically parried for a corner by young Itumeleng Khune.

A minute later, it was the visitors' Aime Kitenge's turn to prove his worth, when he bravely saved David Obua's threatening shot.

From that moment on, the game was a ding-dong battle, with both sides creating, but missing chances and it was difficult to predict who would draw first blood.

However, Obua could have put Kaizer Chiefs ahead in the 41st minute, after a good move initiated by Tshabalala, but the left-footed Ugandan International was not confident enough to kick with his right foot and allowed the visitors' defence to regroup.

The halftime score was 0-0, much to the disappointment of the fans.

Having started the game playing with a lone striker, and in an attempt to reinforce his striking force, in the second half Kaizer Chiefs assistant coach, Fani Madida, deputising for Mushin Etrugal, who watched the game from the stands because of a suspension, introduced Mabhudi Khenyeza, Michael Nkambule, and Kaizer Motaung Junior in place of Tshabalala, Mooki, and Phala.

However Royal Zulu were the first to threaten when Djiehouha tested Itumeleng Khune, but in the interim was adjudged to have fouled Derrick Spencer.

It came as no surprise when Djiehoua burst the bubble in the 56th minute. Kaizer Chiefs' defence was caught square, and after a defence-splitting pass, the former Kaizer Chiefs reject kept his composure before picking his spot to put his side in the lead. That was surely a goal that left Etrugral wondering why he released the big striker at the beginning of the season.

The predator-like Djiehouha was again on target in the 61st minute, but his shot was saved by the alert Khune. Djiehoua was later replaced by Clement Mazibuko in the 77th minute.

Chiefs never rested and the Phefeni boys attacked from all angles but were unlucky when Onismor Bhashera supplied a beautiful cross from the left, but Obua's header hit the upright.

With 10 minutes remaining, Thanda Royal Zulu played a defensive game, and it was difficult for the not-so-glamour boys to penetrate.

The win will see Thanda Zulu Royal moving from 14th position to 11th with 19 points on the log, and Chiefs dropping to fourth from the bottom with 18 points. – Sapa

End of an era as Bernard Parker leaves Chiefs

Mahlatse Mphahlele SPORTS REPORTER 03 June 2022

The massive clear-out at Kaizer Chiefs has claimed veteran attacker Bernard Parker.

Amakhosi, who recently confirmed Arthur Zwane as coach to replace Stuart Baxter, announced on Friday that the contract of the former Bafana Bafana striker will not be renewed when it expires at the end of the month.

This week, Chiefs confirmed the departures of Daniel Cardoso, Lebogang Manyama, Lazarous Kambole, Daniel Akpeyi, Samir Nurković, and Kearyn Baccus and goalkeeper coach Lee Baxter.

Amakhosi are in another rebuilding phase after an unprecedented seventh campaign without silverware in 2021-2022.

Chiefs have already confirmed the off-season signings of Stellenbosch duo centreback Zitha Kwinika and striker Ashley du Preez.

Zwane, assistant Dillon Sheppard and sporting director Kaizer Motaung Jr are expected to announce more signings and player clear-outs in the 2022-2023 preseason.

"His exceptional talent and leadership helped Amakhosi to win four major trophies, including two league titles. His professionalism, both on and off the field, is an objective example to any aspiring young footballer.

"Thank you for your great service and dedication to the club, 'Hond'. You remain a true legend."

'Kaizer Chiefs did the right thing keeping Bernard Parker.'

03 June 2022 - 14:42 BY MARC STRYDOM- TimesLIVE

Former Kaizer Chiefs star Stanton Fredericks says he would have also retained Bernard Parker amid the club's big clear-out this week, "without blinking".

It was conspicuous that as Amakhosi cleared out eight big-name late-20 and 30-somethings this week, taking a broom to the squad after an unprecedented seven seasons without a trophy, the one player many fans have been calling for an exit was retained.

A section of Chiefs' supporters have been baying for 36-year-old Parker to be culled, though others — like the procession of coaches who recognise the playmaker's class and continue to field him — note his contribution.

Fredericks said that contribution, in terms of Parker's often unheralded intelligence on the field and the effect off it as a role model to younger players, is "immense".

"Without blinking I would keep Bernard Parker," Fredericks told TimesLIVE.

"I never played with Bernard Parker, but I can see from afar the presence and the effect he has on the team. And different coaches come in and they keep him, so that tells you.

"I was privy to a conversation when Gavin Hunt had his first training session [as coach of Chiefs in 2020-2021]. From a distance, Gavin was like, 'Who's that player?' And that player was Bernard Parker.

"Because you know what you're going to get from him, even if you think his legs are gone.

"What fans don't understand is that in a squad you need a Bernard Parker — a leader who will set the example. When there's a meeting you arrive 20 minutes before, when there's training you give 100%.

"He's played abroad and locally, he's run the race, and if you're looking to build a young team you need those youngsters to be around a Parker.

"If I draw from my own experiences, I was around John 'Shoes' Moshoeu. And the fact that Shoes would arrive before me at training would make me not allow that and it would force me to come earlier.

"I would not leave before Shoes had left the training session and he used to put in another 30 minutes. The Shoes Moshoeus of this world are so important in big teams.

"So, for me with Parker, I can go on all day and I don't even know this boy personally, but he's definitely somebody I would keep in there.

"Even if he's not going to play 30 games — if Parker is going to start 10 games and come on as a sub in another seven, I would keep him."

Parker netted four goals in 24 DStv Premiership games for the fifth-placed Chiefs in 2021-2022.

Parker's decision shows Kaizer Chiefs' ruthless side, who's next?

Anthony McLennan 03 Jun 2022

The former Bafana Bafana striker and Amakhosi skipper spent 11 years at the club, playing 359 matches, scoring 62 goals, and winning two league titles and two cups.

Kaizer Chiefs suggested they are serious about a complete rebuild after announcing Bernard Parker's departure on Friday. Change of guard.

Parker's immense contribution at Chiefs should earn him respect. But everything comes to an end at some stage and his departure sends the strongest of messages to the rest of the players, everyone within the club, and the supporters - a new broom is clearing away the cobwebs and there will no longer be a place for sentiment and niceties.

For all his professionalism and the example he brought to the younger players, Parker's influence as a striker was fading and he effectively became a utility player last season, occupying several roles. At 36 years old, it was just the right time to close that chapter and for the club to show their intentions of looking to the future. Perhaps Parker may return to Chiefs in another capacity one day.

Parker's departure followed the news earlier this week that Amakhosi have parted ways with Samir Nurkovic, Daniel Cardoso, Lazarous Kambole, Daniel Akpeyi, Kearyn Baccus, Leonardo Castro, and Lebogang Manyama, and then after that, Dumisani Zuma.

The first group of departures were all announced together, followed a few days later by Zuma and then Parker. Which suggests that Chiefs' chop may not be over.

So, who else could be in danger of the chop, if any?

BREAKING | Bernard Parker to leave Kaizer Chiefs- Jun 3, 2022 - 03:30 By Staff reporter

Veteran attacker Bernard Parker is set to leave Kaizer Chiefs with the club deciding against renewing his contract at the club bringing to an end an 11-year spell at the Soweto giants.

The Bafana Bafana international joined the Glamour Boys in 2011, from Eredivisie side, FC Twente and went on to make 359 appearances for the club.

The 36-year-old scored 62 goals for Chiefs and proved a versatile servant for the club where he fulfilled various roles from an out-and-out striker to midfielder.

"Kaizer Chiefs will sadly not renew Bernard Parker's contract when it expires at the end of June 2022," the club said in a statement.

"Parker, a bona fide Kaizer Chiefs legend, will leave the Club he has served with distinction for 11 years.

"He joined Chiefs in 2011 from the Eredivisie side, FC Twente, and his glittering career saw him play 359 matches for Amakhosi and found the net 62 times.

"His exceptional talent and leadership helped Amakhosi to win four major trophies, including two league titles. His professionalism, both on and off the field, is an objective example to any aspiring young footballer.

"Thank you for your great service and dedication to the Club, 'Hond'. You remain a true legend."

Bernard Parker to leave Kaizer Chiefs as an absolute Amakhosi legend!

By Ernest Makhaya 22-05-2022

Bernard Parker will leave Kaizer Chiefs, whenever that is, as an absolute legend after giving his all for the club since his arrival in 2011.

Head coach Arthur Zwane has finally issued a key update on Parker's future with a shocking suggestion.

Bernard Parker will leave Kaizer Chiefs, whenever that is, as an absolute legend after giving his all for the club since his arrival in 2011.

The veteran player, who is 36 years old, has been with Chiefs for 11 years now, and while there is talk of him leaving Naturena, that will not erase his legacy at the club.

On Saturday, Parker netted Amakhosi's equaliser in the 2-2 draw at home against Swallows – and thus, helping Chiefs avoid defeat.

It was Parker's fourth goal of the season for Chiefs, and he netted those goals in 24 league matches while also registering two assists.

BERNARD PARKER FURTHER CEMENTS KAIZER CHIEFS' LEGENDARY STATUS

By scoring against Swallows, Parker took his tally of goals for Chiefs to 62 across all competitions since his arrival.

Parker scored the 62 goals in over 363 competitive matches for Amakhosi – and he is the club's all-time goalscorer in the PSL era.

Behind him is Siphiwe Tshabalala with 58 goals while Knowledge Musona is sitting third in the all-time goalscoring charts with 40 goals.

Former Chiefs striker Collins Mbesuma is behind the trio with 36 goals for the club – the Zambian scored 36 goals between 2003-2005.

Chiefs Announce Departure of Veteran Attacker- Jun 3, 2022 -By Soccer Laduma

Kaizer Chiefs have announced the departure of a veteran attacker after 11 years at the club.

Bernard Parker's contract is set to expire at the end of June 2022 and the club has opted against renewing it.

The 36-year-old's exit is the ninth player departure announced by the Soweto giants in the last three days.

In a statement, Chiefs said; "Kaizer Chiefs will sadly not renew Bernard Parker's contract when it expires at the end of June 2022. Parker, a bona fide Kaizer Chiefs legend, will leave the club he has served with distinction for 11 years."

Parker, who joined Amakhosi back in 2011 from the Eredivisie side, FC Twente leaves Naturena having made 359 appearances with 62 goals to his name. He clinched four major trophies, including two league titles.

"His professionalism, both on and off the field, is an object example to any aspiring young footballer. Thank you for your great service and dedication to the Club, 'Hond'. You remain a true legend".

Parker joined Chiefs in 2011 following his return from abroad where he also made a name for himself.

He leaves Chiefs having lifted four trophies between 2013 and 2015 – Parker was instrumental as he netted the only goal of the game against SuperSport United in the 2013 Nedbank Cup final.

Parker departs as an Amakhosi legend as he's their all-time goalscorer in the PSL era with 62 goals across all competitions.

Parker: Nkosi worked his socks off-Apr 23, 2013 By KickOff

Parker scored a brace as **Amakhosi came from behind to beat the Birds 3-1 in the 'other' Soweto Derby**, but in a generous gesture, he handed his DStv Walka to teammate Nkosi after the game.

"I thought [Nkosi] did very well for us in the heart of midfield," Parker tells Chiefs' official website. "He worked his socks off and was a box-to-box player for us winning balls in the heart of midfield and also was instrumental in some of our attacks.

"'Siya' had not played a lot of games going to the Swallows game, but his performance showed on Saturday that he is one of the important players in the team. I felt on Saturday I did not deserve the man of the match award, he did, that is why I gave him the award."

Parker still leads the scoring charts on 12 goals but had only scored once for Chiefs this year, before the brace against Swallows. He insists, however, that this did not worry him as "the team was still winning".

The striker adds that despite the attitude of some fans to some individual players, his gesture proves that the team is "closer" than ever.

"The spirit in this squad is amazing and we all get along," he says. "We are family. I spoke to Siya a couple of weeks ago when we all felt that the fans were not fair to him. I told him to focus on doing his best and work harder.

"He told me that when he gets another chance he will grab it with both hands. We are really pleased to see him doing so well. He was of course very happy when I presented him with the man of the match award after the game."

My last game against Swallows was on the 21 May 2022 I scored the equaliser in the 85th minute to make the score 2-2. That was memorable.

On his arrival at Kaizer Chiefs Village, Naturena, Bernard Parker said; "Joining Kaizer Chiefs is a realisation of a childhood dream. I am happy to be here, and I am going to give 100 percent every time I get to don the Gold and Black jersey."

Chiefs had long wanted Bernard Parker, who made a name for himself in the football world when he banged in a brace during the FIFA Confederations Cup held in South Africa in 2009. The Reiger Park-born striker joined the Glamour Boys with a reputation for scoring goals, and it is that reputation that took him to Red Star Belgrade in Serbia in 2009 and FC Twente the same year until June 2011. Parker remains a key player in the Amakhosi front unit and is expected to spearhead Kaizer Chiefs' attack.

Chiefs Striker Blames Supply for His Wait For 50 Goals Nov 30, 2017

I am one of the longest-serving campaigners in the Premier Soccer League (PSL), and all-time Kaizer Chiefs striker Bernard Parker reveals the Soweto giants showed interest back in 2009 before his departure to Serbia, saying he is not thinking about hanging up his boots yet.

Having joined the Naturena-based club in 2011, the veteran Amakhosi attacker claims he would be on the scoresheet regularly if he is played as an outright striker, saying it was difficult growing up in a shack in Reiger Park.

'Die Hond' says his longevity in the game is due to the lessons he learned at the School of Excellence, where he was taught to work hard on his shortcomings to fine-tune his skills.

"Chiefs approached me before I left [for Serbia]. I even came for a tour of Chiefs' village [in Naturena], but I kept my promise that I'd come back," Parker told the City Press print edition.

"I haven't even thought about retirement because I'm still going strong. My game's more about mental fortitude and calculating the right moves."

Speaking about his qualities, where he has been a key figure for the PSL table-toppers, the former Bafana Bafana striker added that he's not a special player.

"I'm not a special player, but I was taught three things at the School of Excellence: work on what I lack, work on my weaknesses, and polish my positives," added the former Red Star Belgrade player.

"If I can go back and play as an outright striker, I'll definitely be on the scoresheet."

Looking back at his humble beginnings in a small township in the East Rand [Ekurhuleni], the 34-year-old hitman credits his former schoolteacher Denzel Bezuidenhout for laying a foundation in his career.

"It was difficult growing up in Reiger Park because it's an environment of crime, gangsterism, and drugs," he continued.

KAIZER CHIEFS RELEASE EIGHT PLAYERS, PARKER SURVIVES

As The South African website reported this week, the mighty Amakhosi made their intentions clear. No less than eight footballers were shown out of the Naturena gate.

The list left millions of fans questioning why the 36-year-old Parker's name was not included in the departing group.

Well, Parker carries a lot of value that is not easy to spot on the pitch.

FIVE REASONS PARKER IS GOING NOWHERE

As fans, sometimes we need to be able to see things in perspective when everything is not going well or when the club makes unpopular decisions.

As the people that work closely with the players every day, clubs know better than us.

Here is why Parker is staying with the Soweto giants:

1. Carry club culture in the dressing room

You can always go ahead and sign all the exciting young talent the world has to offer, but you will always need one or two long-serving players to carry the club's culture in the camp, especially at a club with a rich heritage like this one.

2. Tactical wizard

Former club coach **Ernst Middendorp** revealed the reason why every coach has been picking the Boksburg-born Parker: Nobody in the Kaizer Chiefs team can translate and manage tactics on the pitch like 'Die Hond.'

There have also been some confirmations from the club that Parker is a budding future coach who has already begun his studies.

3. Model professional

In a country that is subject to relentless ill-discipline among professional players at training and off the pitch, Parker is known as a model professional and exemplary leader.

4. Experienced mentor

Players, especially young players, do not always have access to the coach's messages and mentorship. To get a message, you just need it from a teammate sometimes. Parker is that character with 18 years in the game, including spells in Europe, and a decade at Naturena.

5. Long-serving loyalty

Playing for Bafana Bafana for all those years and delivering 60 goals and 40 assists in over 300 games for Amakhosi, there's always been tempting offers to leave for better contracts elsewhere, but Parker showed his loyalty.

So, there you have it, releasing Parker was never on the table for the Glamour Boys unless the veteran player requested to exit for personal reasons.

Love or hate him, Parker is a Khosi for life and is expected to work at the club after his retirement. Are big signings ahead?

Chiefs have moved quickly to trim their squad, but now have a void to fill. They've already signed Ashley du Preez and Zitha Kwinika, with Siyethemba Sithebe also expected to be announced soon. With a couple of months in the transfer window to go, we'll likely be seeing several new players and perhaps a couple of big stars - there's been speculation around Victor Letsoalo and Bongani Zungu - in among them.

AUTHOR'S SUMMARY

If I must sum up what everyone has said about Bernard Parker, the following are the outstanding characteristics that stood out very greatly about the man:

Dedication, commitment, respect, self-development, hard worker. Gutsy, honest, humble, resilient, never give up, good heart, caring, prayer warrior, loving husband, loving father, family man, no confrontations, visionary, leader, serving leader, generous, passionate, full of life, an open and forthright person, an inspirational leader, a symbol of never giving up, age is but a number, a winning mentality, hates losing, man of all seasons.

Charley Pietersen

PICTURES

BIBLIOGRAPHY

Bernard Parker Relishes Bafana Bafana Return - The Sports Eagle

Mr Mark Gleeson & Mr Richard Maquire Stats on Parker

Parker to boost Bafana (iol.co.za)

Most Educated South Africa Premier Soccer League Player

By Southlight (self-media writer)

Abedi Pele explains why education is important for football players | Soccers (scorers.org)

Bernard Parker: Mental toughness is key in closing stages of the season (msn.com)

Emotional Bernard Parker On Breaking Kaizer Chiefs Record - iDiski Times

Pictures courtesy from KickOff Magazine

Pictures courtesy from Kaizer Chiefs

https://mastersoccermind.com › 18-qualities-a-great captain must have

10 Exciting Life Lessons You Must Learn From Cristiano Ronaldo (winnersstory.com)

https://winnersstory.com/life-lessons-cristiano-ronaldo/

Statement From Kaizer Chiefs On Social Media Platforms-3 June 2022 At 3:23 Pm

Social Media Responses Kaizer Chiefs Supporters After The Announcement That Parker Is No Longer A Chiefs Player

Parker Returns to Play His 30th Soweto Derby - Kaizer Chiefs FC

https://www.kaizerchiefs.com/club/parker-returns-play-his-30th-soweto-derby

Parker on the cusp of Soweto Derby milestone-Mar 3, 2022 - KickOff By Staff Reporter

Kaizer Chiefs news: Parker has an appetite for the Soweto Derby https://www.thesouthafrican.com/sport/soccer/psl

Kaizer Chiefs news: Parker has an appetite for the Soweto Derby

https://www.thesouthafrican.com/sport/soccer/psl by James Richardson

Wikipedia

Why Parker Deserves More Respect-Kickoff January 2022 Number 537 By Hosea Ramphekwa

Parker equals Mooki and Khune - Kaizer Chiefs FC

https://www.kaizerchiefs.com/news/parker-equals.

They Said That About Shabba & Yeye – Baxter-Oct 25, 2021 – Soccer Laduma-By Mazola Molefe

Emotional Parker On Breaking Chiefs Record - iDiski Times

https://www.idiskitimes.co.za/local/emotional-parker-on-breaking-chiefs-record

McGregor congratulates Bernard Parker on Kaizer Chiefs record (kickoff.com)

Thanda Royal Zulu claim revenge (iol.co.za)

End of an era as Bernard Parker leaves Chiefs - SowetanLIVE

https://www.sowetanlive.co.za/sport/soccer/2022-06

'Kaizer Chiefs did the right thing keeping Bernard Parker

https://www.timeslive.co.za/sport/soccer/2022-06

Parker's decision shows Kaizer Chiefs' ruthless side, who's next?

Anthony McLennan 03 Jun 2022

https://www.goal.com/en-za/lists/parker-decision

Bernard Parker To Leave Kaizer Chiefs Jun 3, 2022, *bing.com/news*

Bernard Parker to leave Kaizer Chiefs as an absolute Amakhosi legend! By Ernest Makhaya 22-05-2022

Chiefs Announce Departure of Veteran Attacker-June 3, 2022 -By Soccer Laduma

Parker: Nkosi worked his socks off-Apr 23, 2013 By KickOff

Kaizer Chiefs: Understanding Parker's stay: FIVE solid reasons - SSiTV Africa

https://ssitv.africa/top-trending/kaizer-chiefs-understanding-parkers-stay-five-solid-reasons/

Chiefs Announce Departure of Veteran Attacker-Jun 3, 2022 -By Soccer Laduma

Kaizer Chiefs Release Eight Players, Parker Survives-bing.com/news.

Picture credits

1, 2, 3 Image: @Mzima_Lumkile / Twitter

4 FC Twente Coach Steve McClaren

5, 10, 11, 14 Kaizer Chiefs

6, 9, 13, 16, Kickoff.com

7 snl24.com

8 Samir Nurkovic (left), Daniel Cardoso (second from right), and Lebogang Manyama (right) - pictured with Bernard Parker (second from left) - have been released from the Soweto club. Image: Frennie Shivambu/Gallo Images

12 soccerladuma.co.za

15 Bernard Parker

17 Credit Picture TS Galaxy Bernard Parker and Mr Tim Sukazi owner & Chairman

18 Bernard Parker with Samuel Eto'o

19 The Parker Family Wendy, Bernard Storm and Skye

BERNARD THE FOOTBALLER

Statistics Career

Bernard Parker is a South African professional association footballer who plays as a midfielder or striker for Kaizer Chiefs. Parker started his professional football career playing for Thanda Royal Zulu in the Premier Soccer League, where he made 70 appearances before a one-year loan to Serbian side Red Star Belgrade. He joined Eredivisie side FC Twente in 2009, where he spent a season and a half before being loaned out to Panserraikos in the Greek Super League. During his time in the Eredivisie, Parker won the 2009-10 Eredivisie and the 2010 Johan Cruyff Shield.

Born: 16 Mar 1986 Boksburg, South Africa
Height: 5' 7" (1,70 m)
Team: Kaizer Chiefs (#25)
Weight: 64 kg

Things you didn't know about Bernard Parker

2009: He joined Eredivisie side FC Twente in 2009, where he spent a season and a half before being loaned out to Panserraikos in the Greek Super League.

2010: He played in the 2010 FIFA World Cup, representing South Africa, but the team was eliminated after the group stage.

2010:   He joined Leicester City on trial in December 2010, with a view to a permanent move away from the Dutch club.

2011:   On 18 January 2011, he moved to Panserraikos FC. on loan, to secure extra game time, and returned to FC Twente after the end of the 2010–11 season.

2012:   In the 2012–13 season, Parker scored 12 league goals in 28 matches and finished as runner-up to Katlego Mashego, who had 13, and helped Chiefs to a league and cup double.

2012:   Parker married Wendy Cherry in Ballito, KwaZulu-Natal, on 16 June 2012, at a ceremony attended by 170 guests.

Wikipedia

Early Life
Parker was born and grew up in Reiger Park, a township next to Boksburg, Gauteng. He was quite good in a variety of sports, excelling in short and long-distance running as well as achieving Eastern Gauteng colours in swimming.

Club Career
A product of the School of Excellence, Parker made his debut in the professional ranks for Cape Town's Hellenic FC, later bought and renamed Benoni Premier United. After the club was once again renamed and moved to Durban, he remained with Thanda Royal Zulu FC until early 2009, when he obtained a transfer to European Cup Winners Red Star in Serbia. His stay in Belgrade was cut short after reports that the club had cash flow problems and owed its players salaries.

Parker signed with FC Twente in July 2009, and was a member of the team that won the Dutch 2009-10 Eredivisie. After Twente manager Steve McClaren's move to Bundesliga, Parker failed to convince new coach Michel Preud'homme of his qualities and thus spent the first half of the 2010-11 Dutch season mostly on the bench. He joined Leicester City on trial in December 2010, with a view to a permanent move away from the Dutch club. On 18 January 2011, he moved to Panserraikos FC on loan, to secure extra game time and returned to FC Twente after the end of the 2010-11 season.

After receiving interest from Swedish clubs Malmö FF and Helsingborgs IF, as well as South Africa's Kaizer Chiefs, Parker chose the latter ahead of the other clubs. In the 2012-13 season, Parker scored 12 league goals in 28 matches and finished as runner up to Katlego Mashego, who had 13, and helped Chiefs to a league and cup double. The following season he won the Lesley Manyathela Golden Boot with 10 goals.

Wikipedia

www.ingramcontent.com/pod-product-compliance
Lightning Source LLC
Chambersburg PA
CBHW072002290426
44109CB00018B/2108